YOU ARE THE MYSTERY

YOU ARE
THE MYSTERY

Joan and

David Zink, Ph. D.

iUniverse.com, Inc.

San Jose New York Lincoln Shanghai

YOU ARE THE MYSTERY

Published by iUniverse.com, Inc.

For information address:
iUniverse.com, Inc.
5220 S 16th, Ste. 200
Lincoln, NE 68512
www.iuniverse.com

Originally published by CSA Press

ISBN: 0-595-14713-5

Printed in the United States of America

This book is dedicated to
all our teachers along the way.

"We are luminous beings. We are perceivers. We are an awareness; we are not objects; we have no solidity. We are boundless. The world of objects and solidity is a way of making our passage on earth convenient. It is only a description that we created to help us. We, or rather our reason, forget that the description is only a description and thus we entrap ourselves in a vicious circle from which we rarely emerge in this lifetime. Learn to see whether the description is upheld by your reason or by your will."

from *Tales Of Power*, Carlos
Castenada

Acknowledgements

We wish to express our appreciation to Prentice-Hall, Inc. for permission to quote from Jane Roberts' book, *Seth Speaks*, c. 1972 and also to Warner Communications for permission to quote from Dr. Harmon Bro's book, Edgar Cayce on Dreams, c. 1974.

We are also indebted to Dr. Elmer Green of the Menninger Clinic for the sharing of his research in bio-feedback training, to Dr. Thelma Moss, University of California at Los Angeles, for her help and encouragement in setting up the Kirlian photography project with Dr. Joseph Pizzo, Lamar Physics department, and to Dr. Stanley R. Dean, Miami, Florida, psychiatrist, for his encouragement of our work in consciousness. We also wish to thank David Cammack for his suggestions on the manuscript and contribution to our dream cases.

These acknowledgements in no way suggest endorsement of our opinions. For them we take full responsibility.

CONTENTS

INTRODUCTION

On all sides we hear much today about consciousness, new age thinking, and scientific exploration of the
relationships between mind, body, and spirit. This new
development is a positive response to the crisis of values
in the West which has emerged since World War II. For
centuries dependent on social endorsement of ethical and
spiritual values, Western consciousness now appears to be
moving toward an individual acceptance of certain values
as a consequence of direct spiritual experience and scientific knowledge.

From the individual's point of view this evolution of
Western consciousness poses certain difficulties but simultaneously offers opportunities. On the negative side, there is
greater emphasis on personal responsibility and, because
of the absence of traditional safeguards, greater risks. At
the same time, the new understanding provides a sane way
of escape from the maze of illusory thinking in which many
are caught. There is more freedom to grow. Hence there is
a greater likelihood of an improved society through individual growth. As individuals grow in understanding,
there is the possibility that society at large will follow,
thereby avoiding the accumulated mistakes of the past.

To some it will appear easier to rest in a subjective
non-productive life, in terms, that is, of growth of consciousness. Such an individual rests in a state of Being.
Growth is demanding. As Carl Jung observed, "the cost
of personality is great." Becoming, evolving, is painful,

but a lifetime of being asleep to man's potential is tragic.

It is the purpose of this book to expand our conception of human nature in terms of both ancient theories and present findings at the frontiers of science. Investigations going on all over the country are shedding new light on ancient truths: the old matter-energy split, for instance, is now being seen as a continuum within a whole system of energy.

We have drawn upon our own counseling experiences and Dr. Zink's system of personality, psychointegration. Correlating his study of personality with the Eastern levels of consciousness, he has developed a gateway to awareness that has helped many. The approach has enabled many ordinary people to work out their own growth despite many real obstacles.

Since the writing of the present work, a controversy has arisen over the handling of physiological evidence by an organization teaching one of the techniques of meditation. This debate in no way invalidates the demonstrable value of a centuries-old approach to inner growth. The physiological benefits described are evident in the persons of truly disciplined meditators.

Joan Wilson Zink
David D. Zink, Ph.D.

Chapter I
You Can Control Your Body

Perhaps an important place to begin is at the Menninger Clinic in Kansas. Here in 1970 Swami Rama of Riski-kesh and the Himalayas changed the temperature in areas of his right palm by ten degrees in a bio-feedback demonstration.

At the Menninger Clinic the subject sits in a chair wired for a training session. "Skin" electrodes are glued to the right forearm, two fingers of the right hand, and the back of the head. He wears a special research jacket equipped with a built-in respiration gauge. He watches a feed-back meter which shows muscle tension as he begins to self-induce his muscle tension to zero. When relaxed, he focuses his attention inward away from outside distractions and an electro-encephalograph shows (and feeds back to him) his brain wave rhythm (a function of the central nervous system), muscle tension and body temperature (functions of the peripheral nervous system).

Swami Rama was "wired" for brain waves, respiration, skin potential, skin resistance, heart behavior (EKG), blood flow in his hands, and temperature. With a degree of mental direction of his body in comparison with which most Westerners are amateurs, he changed at a rate of four degrees fahrenheit per minute one area in his right palm to a "rosy red" and another to an "ashen gray" — a recorded ten degrees fahrenheit difference.

A cardiologist and professor at Kansas University Med-

ical Center witnessed the Swami's subsequent attempts to
stop his heart. He described the result of the Swami's
demonstration as "atrial flutter" in which the heart fires
at its maximum rate without either filling the chambers
properly or allowing the valves to work properly.

Dr. Elmer Green, a leading researcher on bio-feedback
and director of the experiments at the Menninger Clinic,
reports that the Swami stopped his heart from pumping
blood for at least seventeen seconds, a feat which he feels
is of major scientific importance. It means that "training
programs for the establishment and maintenance of psychosomatic health" are feasible. Tests have led Dr. Green
to this conclusion: "any physiological process that can be
directed and displayed in an objective fashion to the subject
can be self-regulated in some degree."

Bio-feedback according to physiologist Dr. Barbara
Brown, author of *New Mind, New Body* (1974), is
"the phenomenon of control over internal biologic functions
occurring when information about the function is fed-back
to the person whose biologic activity it is." Blood pressure, blood flow, lymph flow, muscle tension, brain waves,
migraine headaches, cardiac irregularities, peripheral vas-
cular disease, insomnia, epilepsy, asthma, spastics, and
learning problems all have been self-regulated in one laboratory or another.

These exciting developments which show how will can
affect health have come about slowly. As late as ten years
ago, in spite of studies that came out of World War II,
which showed that 40% of all army disability cases orig-
inated from psychosomatic causes, there was still a mind-
body dichotomy, or split, dominating the disciplines of
medicine, psychology, and science in general. The first
suspicions that emotions could cause disease began with
Freud. In 1910 a German doctor, Johannes Schultz, began
a mind-body training later called autogenic training, but
his results were not translated into English until 1959.
Pointing to the possibility of physical and psychological
control, his work was followed by the 1965 discovery of
Dr. Green and others at Menninger's that human will en-

tered the health domain. Some of thirty-three housewives learned to control the temperature in their hands.

Earlier, in 1952, the well-known psychologist Dr. Gardner Murphy, a pioneer in parapsychology, had suggested the use of instruments to look into these functions. In 1967 Dr. Green began using Murphy's suggestions, thereby giving us the first valid evidence that will can affect health as well as those body processes once thought to be beyond the effect of will. In the last five years these findings and their enormous implications have spread across America.

In bio-feedback "intention—the will—can be mentally evoked and applied to a variety of biological actions with molecular specificity," writes Dr. Barbara Brown in her *Saturday Review* article, "Bio-feedback: An Exercise In Self-Control" (Feb. 22, 1975). Voluntary control used to be considered entirely in terms of muscular activity until bio-feedback brought the recognition that higher, complex mental processes could alter the automatic functions, explains Dr. Brown.

"A strange blindness has prevailed in modern science about the role of the mind in the catalog of human activities," she continues. "The failure of the mind sciences to conjecture meaningfully about mind capabilities is easily seen in their indifferent attitude about the way the mind-brain can supervene in what we take to be the automaticity of reflexes. . . Bio-feedback has shown that each automatic control system can be additionally influenced by higher mental activities." Furthermore, the sensory information which "we once thought played a subsidiary role in directing physiological activities," can be mobilized "to assume a primary role," as when muscle tension is controlled from visual information or when the visual is substituted for "visceral information to control heart rate."

"From the beginning mentalists have challenged scientific authority, just as convinced that mind power controls the universe as scientists are that physical order controls man's destiny . . . Mind power has not existed for most scientific authority, even when it fathomed mysteries or became engulfed in momentous ideological conflicts,"

she continues, ''but suddenly, in the Sixties, like a series
of underground nuclear explosions, experiments began
rumbling through the country that presaged perhaps the
greatest medical discoveries of all time. . . . It has become
clear that man may, after all, have a mind resource to
control his own being, down to the most minute fragments
of the physical structure.''

We can see the intricacy of the mind's control in the
experiments at the Brener and Hothersall laboratories where
human beings unconsciously learned to control their heart
rate. Subjects were asked to make a device produce different pitches of sounds by purely mental means; a red-
light signal showed them when they had made ''high tones,''
and a green-light signalled the low. The tone-producing
device was wired to the subjects and it amplified the electrical energy of their own heartbeats, so that when the
tones were high, the heart rate had accelerated and vice
versa. They were not aware that it was their heartbeats
that turned on the tones nor that they were unconsciously
controlling the heart rate in changing the tones.

Perhaps the most dramatic evidence of our recently
understood mental control of the body is found in the bio-
feedback work of Dr. John Basmajian, an Emory University physiologist. A subject's nervous system was connected to a bio-feedback device for monitoring electrical
activity. Within fifteen to twenty minutes normal people
learned to fire a single motor unit (a motor cell and muscle
cell) in muscle tissue so that it could be recorded elec-
trically. Activating one cell independently means that all
other related cells normally involved in muscle tissue must
be at the same time suppressed, Dr. Brown explains. She
has no answers as to how the human mind is able to ac-
complish this extraordinary feat.

This decision-making part of the brain has not been
defined by physiology or anatomy, but Dr. Brown feels
anyone who had experienced hallucinogens or any religious
mystic could give it more recognition. She accuses the ''mind-
scientists'' of trying to keep the mind's power within physical
confines and of setting rigid limitations which have in-

hibited and restricted norms for intelligence and creativity.

Even more lamentable is the effect of these scientific views upon consciousness. An example of this is the case of a young woman who was confined to a mental hospital after telling her husband of a mystical or "peak" experience which she had had. She was later released only when she denied having had the experience. Such a complete failure to understand higher levels of consciousness can be seen with a frightening regularity in the West. But again, change is in the air. Psychiatrists such as Dr. Stanley R. Dean in Miami, Florida are beginning to take a serious medical interest in the more exotic states of consciousness, particularly what Dr. Dean calls "ultra-consciousness," the anciently-known mystical experience. Of particular interest is the current scientific exploration of the exotic Eastern techniques for raising consciousness, such as Kundalini yoga. Studies now being conducted by yogi-scientist-philosopher Gopi Krishna at the All-India Institute of Medical Sciences may eventually explain to us how the subtle bio-energy called "kundalini" is actually the biological basis for creativity, the higher states of consciousness and the mystical state.

In learning to control events in our bodies that we hardly knew existed, many such as Dr. Barbara Brown wonder whether we are reactivating a lost ability, or evolving a new capacity of mind. Dr. Brown conjectured that this control has, most likely, always existed, because of the human mind's agility in learning in a matter of minutes full control of the single cells buried deep in the spinal cord, as in the Basmajian studies. She writes:

> If it has always existed, has our reluctance to recognize it been because the idea that mind can alter physical nature been too over-whelming conceptually to our primitive understanding of the physical order of the universe, or too God-defying, to bring into conscious appreciation? *Is it possible that man has suppressed a higher level of mental function, one that regulates every cell of the body?* [Italics ours]

"What we are learning," says George Leonard in "In

God's Image," (*Saturday Review,* February 22, 1975), in discussing computers versus the human being, is "that human abilities are far more wonderful than we had dreamed."

The hope is that if man can control his involuntary functions as tests at the Menninger Clinic and elsewhere have shown, he can and will be, in the words of Dr. Green, "responsible to a large extent for his own state of health or disease. Perhaps then people will begin to realize that it is not life that kills us, but rather our reaction to it, and that this reaction can be to a significant extent self-chosen."

Certainly the findings of bio-feedback demonstrate once and for all that mind, body, and energy are simply a continuum within a system and not separate as has long been held. This insight is both timely and crucial. As George Leonard puts it in "In God's Image," "our hope lies not in the brain alone or in the mind alone, but rather in mind, body, and spirit rejoined. (How could we have ever conceived of them as different?)" But, in spite of all evidence from bio-feedback of the functional unity of body, brain and mind (that the mind-brain cannot operate without information from the body and vice-versa), science continues the separation. Dr. Barbara Brown charges that science still continues to impose a schizophrenic therapy on problems of illness. Certainly a number of our contemporary attitudes need radical revision.

Bio-feedback also has other important implications. The crutches of environment and heredity that man has been using for the past hundred years and more now begin to break under the weight of scientific pressure. Dr. Karl Menninger, dean of American psychiatry, whose position was once one of a strong environmental determinism as seen in his well-known book of five years ago, *The Crime of Punishment,* has, as a result of bio-feedback experiments, reversed his opinion. Reasoning from the conscious control of involuntary body processes, his latest book *Whatever Became of Sin?* argues that man does have some freedom of choice and therefore *can* be responsible.

When a man is completely a product of his environment and his physiology, then no one is responsible for any aggressive act. In this view, there can be only despair for society and the individual, because change or improvement cannot be expected. On the other hand, the individual can recover his freedom (and responsibility) and the ability to grow, only by realizing that it is possible. These limiting views, our legacy from the early stages of the social sciences, are being undermined by better science.

"We often find it easy to be pessimistic about human prospects," adds George Leonard, "but that pessimism cannot explain why we continually overlook the potential of our species, the awesome capacities of all life on this planet, the even more awesome capabilities of human consciousness. . . . Fearing the brightness of our own potentialities we keep watching the shadows on the wall of the cave, calling the larger vision 'unscientific,' 'soft.' But even that rationalization is being taken away from us. . . . The hardest science is now corroborating the vision of life, body, and mind that the cynics would call 'soft.' We take comfort in the fact that our religions also concede that we are fallen, unsaved, unenlightened. No matter how fallen, however, we can no longer deny our godlike capacities—science will not permit the denial."

For a moment let us briefly review the events which have led man into the widespread scientific determinism of today. Since Darwin's *Origin of Species* in 1859, we have had a concept of human and animal life surviving according to strength and adaptability to environment. Out of this view came sociology's claim that man is largely patterned, as well as determined, by his environment, of which he is usually seen to be a victim. At the turn of the century, this kind of determinism appeared to be reinforced by psychology as Sigmund Freud convinced the world that men were determined by their biological drives. Today we have what seems to be a whole culture fixated at this level of understanding and a world view typified by such books as B.F. Skinner's *Beyond Freedom and Dignity*.

Science has long held to the illusion that its pursuits are value free. This may have been an important assumption during the break away from the church, but it is hardly true in the strict sense. The physical sciences in the nineteenth century, especially biology and geology, among other values, held an anti-theological bias, an orientation which was even more prominent in the newly emerging social sciences, particularly sociology. Whatever the cost for the Western viewpoint and its prolonged effect upon the individual psyche, the bias against the church during the past century was vitally necessary for the development of science. It appears to be analogous to the young person's rebellion against parental authority as he seeks to develop his own identity. Henry David Thoreau, though inspired to his Walden experience by an older man, Emerson, says in *Walden,* "I have lived some thirty years on this planet, and I have yet to hear the first syllable of even earnest advice from my seniors."

Unfortunately, along with the rebellion against the church, there was a focus upon reason which excluded all other modes of perceiving, such as feeling and intuition. Denial of the feelings can have serious consequences. One of the great scientists of the age to which we have just alluded, Charles Darwin, recognized in his *Autobiography* that he had become a machine for grinding general laws out of facts. He then observed the lopsided effect on his personality, especially the diminishing of his ethical nature. With a widespread denial of the feelings through which the Unconscious expresses and guides, we can see the far reaching and grave consequences for Western culture itself.

One twentieth-century consequence of relying exclusively on the rational mode of cognition was noted by Arthur Koestler in his *Darkness at Noon* (1941). The old Bolshevik, Rubashov, one of the founding fathers of the revolution, awaits his appearance in the Moscow purge trials. Pondering what had gone wrong with their beautifully rational and idealist dream, he finally concludes, "We were sailing without ethical ballast." At last he recognizes that the end does not justify the means.

Nuclear weapons, genetic engineering, advances in medical technology, and the conditioning of behavioral psychology all turn our attention to the question of values in science, this time inescapably. The ethical side of generating a nuclear technology came late to a few physicists. Molecular biologists have become also more cautious in their plans to determine the human models of the future, only because of adverse public reaction. In medicine the ethical questions are just being touched upon.

On the positive side, Darwin's *Origin Of Species,* besides launching a new biology, showed the importance of environment upon the survival of various species, and self-conscious Victorians who were burdened with the problems of the Industrial Revolution naturally saw the implications for the human species, upon which we are again focussing today: would man himself survive his own environmental hazards?

The deterministic views in psychology apparently also represent a necessary developmental stage before science gains new data about the psyche. The reason that the rational-empirical (what was acceptable to reason and proven by experience) world view went strongly reinforced and unchallenged for several centuries was due to two ways of thinking: what some psychologists call the rational mode of thought, or logical and verbal reasoning, along with the sensation mode of perception or accepting the evidence of the five senses as the total reality. The recent challenges to this type of consciousness are Jungian psychology, two-brain research, and the findings of parapsychology.

Early in his work, psychiatrist Carl Jung recognized the importance of the unconscious mind, particularly in its correction of the imbalance brought on by the conscious mind. While many still find his work difficult, it is the logical outcome of nearly two centuries of thought in the West. The 19th century romantic writers who emphasized feeling and intuition in England and on the Continent, prepared the way first for Freud's conception of the unconscious and then for Jung's.

In *The Psychology Of Consciousness,* physiologist Dr.
Robert Ornstein connects the verbal-logical type of personality with the scientist, the logician, or the mathematician, those committed to reason and "correct" proof.
The mind untutored by formal education is often the
artist, craftsman, dancer, or the dreamer. The thought
of such persons is often unsatisfactory to the purely rational
mind. These personality differences stem from the structure of the brain. The cerebral cortex of the brain is divided
into two hemispheres, the left side of the body being mainly
controlled by the right side of the cortex, the right side of
the body by the left side. Dr. Ornstein explains that "The
structure and function of these two 'half-brains' in some
part underlie the two modes of consciousness which exist
at the same time in all of us," and in the normal person
the left hemisphere is involved with analytic, logical
thinking, "especially in verbal and mathematical functions"
while the right hemisphere is "primarily responsible for our
orientation in space, artistic endeavors, crafts, body image,
recognition of faces." (p. 51) The right side works in a
more rational, and simultaneous way, integrating many
inputs at once, while the left side of the brain is predom-
inantly analytic and sequential (i.e. it works in sequence),
Ornstein says, summarizing current two-brain research.

These findings have been accumulated through studies
of people whose brains have been damaged by accident
or illness. Observations of tumors, lesions, and lobectomies
which began as long as a hundred years ago have established the apparent functions of the two lobes. In split-
brain patients where the corpus callosum (the bundles of
nerve fibers through which the two sides of the brain communicate) have been severed, it has been found that the
experience of each hemisphere is unique and independent
of the other.

Dr. Ornstein feels that the recognition that we possess
two cerebral hemispheres which are specialized and which
operate in two different ways may help us to understand
the dual nature of our consciousness. Through literature
this duality has been depicted in clashes between reason

and passion, mind and intuition. Freud used the labels the "unconscious" and "subconscious," with the language and rational side being called "conscious," a development which perhaps marks the beginning of contemporary denials of the invaluable contribution of the intuitive mind (or "subconscious" in Freud's terms). The two modes of operation complement each other, but do not readily substitute for one another, says Dr. Ornstein. "It is the polarity and the integration of these two modes of consciousness, the complementary workings of the intellect and the intuitive, which underlie our highest achievements."

Many people are aware that scientific discoveries such as Einstein's theory of relativity and the discovery of the carbon ring have occurred through the intuitive mind or even dream states. Poincare, the French mathematician, tells of receiving an important idea for his work after dismissing it from his conscious mind and going for a drive in the country. We will deal with the amazing guidance of the "unconscious" through dreams in the chapter on dreams. Of his own creative process Albert Einstein said, "the really valuable thing is the intuition."

The late Italian psychiatrist of world renown, Dr. Roberto Assagioli, describes the ideal relationship between the two modes of thinking in his *Psychosynthesis:*

> . . . intuition is the creative advance toward reality. Intellect first performs the valuable and necessary function of interpreting, i.e., of translating, verbalizing in acceptable mental terms, the results of the intuition; second, to check its validity; and third, to coordinate and to include it into the body of already accepted knowledge. These functions are the rightful activity of the intellect . . . . A really fine and harmonious interplay between the two can work perfectly in a successive rhythm: intuitional insight, interpretation, further insight and its interpretation, and so on.

Assagioli has found, especially among intellectuals, that many prevent this ideal functioning within themselves through fear of the intuitive or feeling mode: "They are diffident and treat it very gingerly; consciously or unconsciously, in most cases they repress it.'' We need to recognize that a complete person uses and balances both reason and intuition.

It is interesting to see that the idea of dual consciousness is common in a number of other cultures such as the Hopi Indians, the Buddhists, and in the Chinese Yin-Yang where the Creative is Spirit and the Receptive is Nature. Yet in our culture the Unconscious, as popularized by Freud, until rather recently has been the least understood major psychological formulation of modern times. Even academic psychology is not really at home with the Unconscious. This distrust originally stems from Freud's view of the Unconscious as a sort of psychic garbage can, but contemporary research is changing this opinion. Biofeedback, altered states of consciousness (including hallucinogenics and dream research) are nurturing an emerging new consciousness which includes a profound recognition of the creative importance of the Unconscious.

Another pioneer who is speeding the expansion of the new Western consciousness is Lawrence LeShan, *The Medium, The Mystic, and the Physicist* (1974). LeShan is a researcher in transpersonal psychology, who shows a junction at the frontiers of science and religion, evident in statements by theoretical physicists and modern mystics which come together in theory. His emphasis on paranormal healing includes a training program for healers in which physicians are included.

Because his pioneering work was done in an Air Force Base hospital, Dr. O. Carl Simonton, chief of radiation therapy at Travis Air Force Base from 1971 to 1973 is one of the more courageous contributors to the new consciousness. His imaginative breakthrough in the treatment of cancer is reviewed in Dr. Jean Shinoda's ''Meditation and Psycholgy in the Treatment of Cancer,'' (*Psychic,* 1973). ''The mind, the emotions and the attitudes of a patient play a role in both the development of a disease, cancer included, and the response that the patient has to any form of treatment,'' Dr. Simonton says. This treatment includes cobalt radiation, psychotherapy sessions which include the patient's friends and relatives (to strengthen the will to live), and a meditation technique which involves relaxation and the visualization of the proper operation of the immune mechanism. Over a two-year period with one-hundred and fifty patients, improvement or non-improvement was correlated with the degree of the patient's participation and positive or negative attitude. Among the patients who wished to recover Dr. Simonton had an amazing number of cures.

Here we can see several factors working together to return the body to a healthy state: the will to live, meditation and relaxation with health suggestions being fed into the unconscious by the conscious mind, visualization and faith.

One of the most dramatic examples of the importance of faith is given in a *Science of Mind* article (Dec. 1974). In "Faith vs. Cancer," Dr. Phillip West describes the complete disappearance of cancer in a terminal case and its reappearance as faith in the drug being used was weakened. In this particular case the patient had, both a very strong will to live, and faith in a miracle drug named Krebiozen. "When he heard we were going to begin treatment with Krebiozen, his enthusiasm knew no bounds," Dr. West writes. Given the drug, though other patients showed no change, the patient in question improved brilliantly. "Incredible as it sounds, this 'terminal' patient gasping his last breath through an oxygen mask, was now not only breathing normally and fully active, he took off in his plane and flew at 12,000 feet with no discomfort," Dr. West continues.

Then came conflicting reports and releases to the news as to the ineffectiveness of the drug and as the patient's faith waned, he returned, after two months of perfect health, to his original state. Dr. West then, for scientific reasons, took advantage of the patient's innate optimism and gave him water injections of what he called a "super-refined, double strength version" of the drug. "Recovery from his second near-terminal state was more dramatic than the first," his physician writes. The patient might be alive

today had not an AMA announcement of the drug's worth-
lessness completely crumpled his hopes. He then succumbed
in a few days after being admitted to the hospital.

No doubt the will to live influences the very cells of our
bodies, speeding the mechanisms by which they return to
a healthy state. Mrs. B. feels that her will power aided
greatly a recovery which might have been a lengthy one.
Hurt in an automobile accident, Mrs. B. was facing a long
hospital stay. She had suffered a broken pelvis, two broken
thighs, and the roof of her mouth was split. With indomin-
able spirit she refused to stay in the hospital past several
days and upon returning to her large family, she removed
the cast from her body with a razor blade. She stayed
in a wheelchair during a period of recuperation which she
believes was shortened by her belief and will. Today she
walks with absolutely no trace of a limp.

Today we hear much about the process of visualization
in the treatment of disease. Probably one of the most profound cases illustrating its effectiveness is that of Evelyn
Monahan, Special Studies Instructor at Georgia State University in Atlanta. In her early twenties, Miss Monahan
fell on a slippery floor and damaged the occipital area
of her brain. She lost her sight in a closing down of vision
called "tunnel vision" and doctors believed she would never
see again. Added to this, as a result of the fall, was the
onset of epilepsy and, in spite of Dilantin and pheno-
barbital, she often had as many as twelve seizures a day.
A final difficulty occurred when a doctor, draining an
abcess on her neck, severed the spinal accessory nerve
which left her left arm paralyzed. After nine years, which
must have been constant torture, Evelyn asked two friends
who were gifted in visualization to work with her. The
news of her dramatic recovery was covered by the 1973
International issue of *Time* magazine. In her astonishing
case, sight returned within five days of the start of the
visualizing process undertaken by the three women. Within
ten days she had regained the use of her arm. At this
time an EEG showed that her brain waves were normal.
"Through the use of psycho-kinetic healing, more commonly

known as mind over matter, my two friends and I were able to tap the God-force available to each person and bring about a complete healing in each case," she writes.

In the fascinating teaching from Seth in *Seth Speaks*, by Jane Roberts, we are reminded that *thought creates the reality*. Seth says, "This characteristic of materializing thoughts and emotions into physical realities is an attribute of the soul. This knowledge—that your universe is idea construction— can immediately give you clues that enable you to change your environment and circumstances beneficially. The more intense your imagination and inner experience, therefore, the more important it is that you realize the methods by which this inner experience becomes physically real. Your thoughts and emotions begin their journey into physical actualization at the moment of conception." When your thoughts are creative and optimistic, your suppositions will come quickly to pass.

We do not need to take Seth's word, if we do not wish. We can, instead, turn to parapsychology where demonstrations that mind can affect and even move matter began with Nelya Kulagina of Russia. Millions have watched on television as she moved objects with the energy of her mind. Duke University experiments proved some years ago that mind could affect the throw of dice. Telepathic messages received in scientific tests show that thoughts can go through steel and other shielding as well as travel great distances simultaneously. Persons receiving messages were monitored for brain waves, heart rate, etc. which showed changes corresponding to the time and intensity of the received thought.

There are hosts of others arising to make sure that we do not under-estimate the mind's power. Uri Geller, the young man from Tel Aviv, can bend forks and stop watches. Ingo Swann can change the temperature of objects inside of vacuum bottles. Olga Worrall has, in a test at Agnes Scott College, caused turbulence in a Wilson cloud chamber there from a distance of 600 miles away. In Japan a twelve-year old, Jun Sekiguchi, bent two spoons double and broke a third, apparently dissolving .03 grams of metal in the process. No one who is at all abreast of today's developments in parapsychology can deny logically the power of the mind, and that is why we must be careful with the habitual ways we think about others and ourselves.

In comparing the human being to the computer, George Leonard writes in "In God's Image," "What we are learning is not that computers are any less wonderful than we had imagined but that human abilities are far more wonderful than we had dreamed." *Saturday Review* science editor, Albert Rosenfield, in describing the new consciousness, mind research, and the human potential writes, "The 'mind' they speak of is . . . an integrated unity. It is body-brain, psyche-soma, matter-spirit. Even our surroundings are envisioned as part of the self."

One of the first laboratories whose work may tell us more about the matter-spirit relationship than any other is that of Russians, Semyon and Valentina Kirlian, who, in demonstrating a scientifically repeatable photographic technique for filming the energy fields around all living creatures, may have given the world as important a discovery as Einstein's theory. Mystics, clairvoyants and Yogis have claimed for ages that the physical body is surrounded by a non-physical counter-part. Russian biologist V.M. Inyushin, who worked with the Kirlians in 1968 used the term "bioplasma body" for the aura and said that it was similiar or identical to the "aura" or "astral body" defined in Yogic literature.

The human aura has been recorded by medieval painters as a halo effect, and electrical discharges in the form of bluish flames are as old as the burning bush on Mt. Sinai (Ex. 3-2) and the flames of Pentecost (Acts 2:3), Stanley Krippner, author of *The Kirlian Aura: Photographing the Galaxies of Life* reminds us. The general phenomenon has been recorded since the dawn of recorded time, hovering around ships' masts, church towers and airplane wing tips. The man responsible for developing alternating current, Nikola Tesla unknowingly created "St. Elmo's fire" by producing with giant coils, banks of condensers and other apparatuses, the first man-made lightning. At the turn of the century, Tesla stood in an electrical field and had photographs taken which showed sparks radiating from his body. In 1898 a Russian engineer and electrical researcher Yakov Narkevich-Todko demonstrated "electro-graphic photos obtained with the help of quiet electrical discharges," Krippner writes.

It was not, however, until 1911 that an English doctor Walter Kilner decided to inquire into the aura. With the use of dicyanin dye screens to sensitize the rods of his eyes, Kilner slowly learned in a darkened room to see the shapes around his patient's bodies. His work *The Human Atmosphere: or the Aura Made Visible by the Aid of Chemical Screens,* was further extended by another man trained in science and medicine, Oscar Bagnall who in 1937 published *The Origin and Properties of The Human Aura.*

Semyon Kirlian began developing his photographic process by noticing sparks flashing from the skin of a patient receiving electrotherapy. He and his wife Valentina developed a process which bears their name, which uses a high-voltage alternating current energy field between two condenser-like plates. "Our work showed that in a high-frequency field, auto-electrons and auto-ion emission is characteristic of all bodies of nature including living organisms," Krippner quotes the Kirlians as saying.

The Kirlians found that all objects photographed by the "Kirlian" process, produced an effect similar to the corona of the sun around the edges of the moon during a total eclipse. But the living objects produced colored flares, flashes and bubbles. The photographs show the physical, chemical and dynamic characteristics of the object. Each species of a plant photographed under the same conditions gave an image of a special character. Maize and a geranium leaf had differing patterns; wheat always resembled the wheat pattern etc. "Absolutely inert and totally brute matter does *not exist,*" wrote the great paleontologist and theologian Teilhard de Chardin. "Every element of the universe contains, at least to an infinitesimal degree, some germ of inwardness and spontaneity, that is to say consciousness, it can be imperceptible but still does exist." One of the Kirlians' first exciting discoveries was that of the energy pattern shown by the Kirlian photograph. Dr. Harold Burr at Yale in 1935, called this pattern an "energy field" and in his book *The Fields of Life* (1972) believed that the energy system determined the form of the organism. Besides its immense relevance to medical diagnosis, the filming of these patterns may tell us much about the basis of life when finally understood.

In the dramatic work of polygraph expert, Cleve Backster, with grocery store eggs, Mr. Backster found that wired eggs gave evidence of a heart beat before any circulatory system was evident upon dissection. The energy field surrounding the egg obviously existed prior to the forming of the embryo itself. Can the energy system then be the formal cause or first cause, and can it be correlated with a form of consciousness independent of the physical or material body? Again Teilhard de Chardin's words are applicable: "Matter and consciousness are bound together," he says, "in the sense that it (consciousness) becomes organically and physically rooted in the same cosmic process. . . ." He saw it not as something strange or fortuitous, but as a phenomenon connected with "the drift of cosmic matter—toward increasingly high molecular groups."

Kirlian work in Russia, at U.C.L.A. and elsewhere with the phantom leaf certainly suggests that this is so. Dr. Thelma Moss and Ken Johnson at U.C.L.A. in their work *The Probability Of the Impossible* (1974), exhibit Kirlian photographs of the pattern of a whole leaf still intact though the tip has been severed. The "phantom" has also been filmed in South America and by Richard Miller of Seattle. Perhaps this amazing fact explains how animals can regenerate an amputated limb.

The energy field appears, then, to be the necessary first step in forming a physical body. Mystics and clairvoyants would agree that this is so. The consciousness of each living thing is perhaps carried in the energy body, which is perhaps also the soul. Changes in the energy body take place before being evident in the physical form. This was the basic principle of acupuncture among the ancient

Chinese doctors. A healthy mind and body were obtained by keeping the energy system intact and functioning as a whole. Even today Kirlian photography shows energy fleeing from fingertips when the subject is tired, injured, or mentally disturbed, and at or before death, of course, all of the energy radiation gradually flows out.

Acupuncture has also been immensely successful in treating the symptoms of phantom limb pain. Treatment of the opposite limb somehow affects the energy balance. The mere fact of pain remaining in the area where a limb has been amputated should tell us something if we are really curious.

Though the basic question of what is being filmed here is still unanswered, Kirlian work which we have conducted at Lamar University for the past three years can offer certain fairly definite suggestions. For one thing, the points at which the energy flares coincide with the acupuncture points. A Kirlian profile of a face, done for the first time in the U.S. at our laboratory, shows an energy flare in the cheek at the beginning point of the gall-bladder meridian. Dr. Thelma Moss has verified the acupuncture points in our Kirlian profile with the help of a medical doctor from Hong Kong. Changes in emotional states have also been ascertained. Students filmed in a deeply spiritual state show large and beautiful coronas of light around their fingertips. Those who are upset show irregular patterns and the introvert's fingertip aura is small. Tests made elsewhere demonstrate structural differences between the fingertip photograph of a schizophrenic before and after chemical treatment, when the corona around the fingertip becomes more regular.

Not only does the light pattern vary according to the health and emotional state of the subject, but the color also changes. A photograph from our lab taken before and after cobalt therapy in a cancer case showed a change in structure and color. A well-known contemporary poet, well acquainted with the chakras of Eastern philosophy (considered energy vortices in the energy body), concentrated on each chakra in succession from the crown chakra at the top of the head to the base of the spine, and showed a range of colors descending from blue to red. As we know, blue light is a much higher frequency than red. In the Eastern tradition, the higher chakras relate to higher levels of consciousness, lower chakras to lower levels of consciousness. Thus our Kirlian work suggests the validity of these esoteric traditions.

In her fascinating work with the super-sensitive or psychics, psychiatrist Dr. Shafica Karagulla has reported on sensitives who could not only see the electrical pattern in the human brain, but the colors of the emotions as well. These colors form part of the knowledge of the ancient mystery religions as well as of the Eastern religions of today: red seems to be equated with anger or the base emotions, blue with spirituality, yellow with intelligence, gray and dulled colors with depression.

Some traditions teach that man has other "bodies" than the physical fields of energy which overlap the area around him. These are: the etheric double which extends one-fourth of an inch around the body like an envelope and which is electrical and has to do with feeling pain or cold (which may explain why the amputated limb can still register pain), the astral which has to do with the passions, emotions, and sensations, the mental which determines or reflects intelligence, and the seat of the soul or causal body. Perhaps students of the ancient traditions would say that what is being filmed in Kirlian photography is the etheric or vital body, with some of the emotional and mental states also being indicatd.

Dr. Thelma Moss of U.C.L.A. found that alcohol and drugs affected the fingertip aura significantly, while hands placed in hot or cold water before filming made little difference. States induced by relaxation, meditation, and Yogic breathing showed an expansion of the aura. Auras of faith healers diminished gradually as the aura of the patient receiving the healing grew, a transfer of energy clearly taking place. Scratched and mutilated leaves held in the hands of healers increased in brightness after being treated.

According to Robert J. Fuller, Mankind Research Unlimited (MRU) is finding funding for Kirlian photography. The Department of Defense and the Department of Transportation are considering the use of Kirlian photographs to identify potential sky-jackers and assassins who might register high-anxiety states. Gerald Jampoloshy of the Child Center in Kentfield, California is planning to use the Kirlian photograph with dying patients to see when the unconscious decision to stop living is made. According to Stanley Krippner, studies of persons in a hypnotic state reveal that unconscious decisions do affect the aura.

Kirlian photographs have demonstrated that a reddish blur occured in the auras of six people at Santa Rosa Junior College for six to twenty-four hours before they exhibited the symptoms of the London flu.

"The news is," writes Albert Rosenfield, science editor of *Saturday Review,* "that many bona-fide, faultlessly credentialed scientists have opened up their minds—and more importantly their labs—to areas of research that they would formerly have considered out of bounds." And, as should be evident, the results are mind-expanding. Perhaps the greatest jolt to the human mind is the way in which some research has extended consciousness to plants and animals. For Teilhard de Chardin, brute matter does not exist. That all life has a portion of consciousness is shown in detail in the above mentioned experiments of Cleve Backster. A polygraph expert, Backster began by wiring up his dracaena. He discovered that the plant registered emotional peaks when he thought of burning a leaf. Later he found that plants in one room "reacted emotionally" at the exact instant that brine shrimp in another room were dropped into boiling water. The moment of death of the shrimp was registered by the plants, though separated by space and a faraday screen.

Chardin explained that we are all a part of an organic whole, that "no elemental thread in the universe is independent in its growth of its neighboring thread." Through his study of palentology, he formed an idea of life moving in a definite direction, a steady rising curve of life, living creatures thrusting toward a more sensitive and elaborate

nervous system, the phenomenon of evolving consciousness of more and more complicated elements. The threads
or chains of elements from which all grow represent a
naturally ordered series in which the links "can no more
be exchanged than can the successive states of infancy,
adolescence, maturity and senility in our lives."

In man he found an extreme physico-chemical complexity which led him to consider him the most highly
synthesized form of matter known in the Universe. He
felt man had an extreme degree of organization which made
him the most perfectly and deeply centered of all cosmic
particles, with psychic development (reflection and thought)
which places him head and shoulders above all other conscious living things known to us.

In man it is not the quantity of corpuscles in his body,
but that the millions of cells in his brain have reached a
maximum of linked complication and a centralized organization that makes him significant.

Julian Huxley declared man as the "highest, the richest,
the most significant object within range of our investigations,
because it is in him that cosmic evolution is culminating
at this moment, having become, by our reflection, conscious of itself."

In the scientific work surveyed above, we can begin to
see the awesome complexity and capabilities of the human being. What is so very important now is for the human participant himself to realize and reflect upon his
own potential for growth and accomplishment in the unfolding drama of contemporary life.

Chapter II
Your Emotional Problems and
How to Deal With Them

We are in the midst of a consciousness revolution.
"The frontier territories being explored bear such names
as The New Consciousness, Mind Research, The Human
Potential," writes Albert Rosenfield, science editor of *Saturday Review*. Describing the new ground as "grandiose in
its scope, exuberant" and invested with "a shared sense of
urgency," Rosenfield says that its "major goal is to expand human awareness, to convince us that we are greater
than we think we are—as great as we will let ourselves become."

Some will doubtless stop and point accusing fingers
at the widespread human failure evident on every hand.
Have we really come very far? Aren't we generally on a
downward slope? On the contrary, while the average man
may yet be unaware of it, change is already here. Man,
in his disillusionment, is turning away from the outside
world and its seemingly unsolvable problems for a closer
look at himself. This inward looking is the prerequisite
by which a new orientation and growth can and does
occur. And science is showing the way.

In laboratories across the country experiments in bio-
feedback, Kirlian photography, and dream research are
coming to our aid. "It is clear that we are operating with
only a tiny fraction of our true abilities," writes George
Leonard in the *Saturday Review* "The pessimism which we
often feel about human prospects cannot explain," he writes,

33

"why we continually overlook the potential of our species, the awesome capabilities of all life on this planet, the even more awesome capabilities of human consciousness." (Feb. 22, 1975)

We need certainly to understand the basis for our pessimism, and the concept of lack and failure which has pervaded our idea of ourselves for generations. Seventeenth and eighteenth-century philosophers such as Descartes and Locke gave man the idea that the individual, his mind and the cosmos were all machines. Only mechanically, working through the five senses, could the mind perceive other minds and the material world itself. Reason was the only way of knowing anything. Consciousness was felt to be largely influenced by biological needs which were often in conflict with society. One had no inner, personal direction. The unconscious mind itself was later considered by Freud and other psychologists as a sort of psychic garbage can. Its positive potential, its natural tendency to wholeness was ignored. Dreams, because of their association with the sub-consciousness, were given no real importance. Altered states of consciousness could only be achieved by chemical means.

The substance of much formal education in the U.S. to date (and probably in the other modern industrial nations as well) has been the type of information which can be most readily used, that acquired by the workings of the "rational mind." In *The Anatomy of Human Destructiveness,* Erich Fromm describes modern man as schizoid because of his imbalance on the rational side. He says that "the cybernetic man is almost exclusively cerebrally oriented: he is *monocerebral man.* His approach to the whole world around him—and to himself—is intellectual; he wants to know what things are, how they function and how they can be constructed or manipulated. This is the approach that has been fostered by science, and that has become dominant since the end of the middle ages. It is the very essence of modern progress, the basis of the technical domination of the world and of mass consumption."

Dr. Fromm finds the malady "ominous" because it appears not only in science but throughout the population and has led to a degradation of feelings: "inasmuch as they (the feelings) are alive, they are not cultivated and are relatively crude: they take the form of passions, such as the passion to win, to prove superior to others, to destroy, or the excitement in sex, speed and noise."

In marked contrast with those sickened by an imbalance on the rational side, Abraham Maslow writes (in *Motivation and Personality*) of personalities which are more whole. In these "self-actualizers" "the age-old opposition between heart and head, reason and instinct . . . was seen to disappear." The self-actualizer approached greater wholeness.

"Consciousness," says Seth, in *Seth Speaks* by Jane Roberts, "is a way of perceiving the various dimensions of reality," but much more. The "new" understanding of consciousness was long ago recognized both in Eastern religions and in Christianity. Generated by the work of Carl Jung and Robert O. Assagioli, today's transpersonal psychologists and parapsychologists are beginning to agree on this larger definition of consciousness. The rational and the feeling modes of knowing are considered valid (as well as the five senses and ESP).

In the emerging new view of consciousness individual minds are not trapped within a skull fed only by the five senses but are instead connected with other minds and the physical universe. They can affect matter (as seen in chapter one). These connections are described as paranormal simply because of our present ignorance, but in the physics and psychology to come, they will be understood as natural phenomena. Clairvoyance, telepathy, and psycho-kinesis will be recognized for their true implications—phenomena which extend to infinity the system in which human beings operate.

What critics of the past "called magic or the occult, we today now recognize as the operation of certain tenuous and imponderable laws that permeate the entire Cosmos," writes Henry C. Roberts. "These intangible but all pervading forces we group today under the general title of 'Extra Sensory Perception.' " With other leading thinkers, Dr.

Thelma Moss, U.C.L.A. physiologist, believes that psi phenomena are peripheral events which happen to an individual who is on his way to transcending space and time.
Dr. Emily Herman in *The Meaning and Value of Mysticism*
states that the appearance of psi phenomena is a function
of the spirit of human beings. As long ago as the eighteenth
century the famed German mystic, Schopenhauer, said,
"The man who denies the fact of clairvoyance is not entitled to be called a skeptic; he is merely ignorant."

In the new view the conscious mind is supervised by the
ego, but beneath the seemingly blank tablet of the mind
at the beginning of life, is an unconscious layer which already has depth and experience. Recent studies in regression
hypnosis and with hallucinogenics tend to confirm the
memories of racial experience which Jung observed in the
study of 80,000 dreams. In this view the intuitive feelings
and dreams can also provide models for right conduct.
Guidance from dreams will be explored in a later chapter.
The validity of both the rational and the feeling modes
of knowing is now being recognized as well as the inter-
play of the five senses and ESP. The important point is
that correction is available from one's own consciousness,
that the Unconscious can become a source of vitality, a
health-giving counterpoise for the conscious mind. The Unconscious is not only a positive complement to consciousness, it is also a channel to transpersonal awareness or
cosmic consciousness which transcends both time and space
as we presently know them.

"It is only because you are so busily concerned with
daily matters that you do not realize that there is a portion
of you who knows its own powers are far superior to those
shown by the ordinary self," says Seth in *Seth Speaks*.
This higher portion of ourselves goes by various names.
In Jungian psychology the Self transcends the ego, as the
Soul does the body in religious views. For the Naskapi
Indians of Labrador, Mista Peo is the name for the inner
self, meaning Great Man.

It is through this divine portion of ourselves that guidance, inspiration, and the creative handling of our lives
and affairs come about. Ralph Waldo Emerson once wrote:

"All true wisdom of thought and action comes of deference to this instinct. To make a practical use of this instinct in every part of life constitutes true wisdom, and we must form the habit of preferring in all cases its guidance, which is given as it is used."

Altered states then are natural in this new (yet ancient) view as the person involved approaches wholeness. Not through artificial means, but through achievement of a balanced personality, through physical health, and by a disciplined meditative process the ego first becomes healthy and eventually becomes subordinated to the Self, or soul-channel. Jung wrote, "In the last analysis every life is the realization of a whole, that is, of a self for which reason this realization can be called 'individuation.' " Finding this wholeness, carrying out this growth process of "individuation" requires spiritual, psychological, and mental growth and we will presently look at some case studies in which individuals have recognized the benefits of such growth.

We are going to divide consciousness into various levels so that the reader can begin to analyze for himself where the major thrust of his own personality or energy lies. In the ideas which follow, we must turn away from an "other-directed personality" approach and look deeply into ourselves, for measuring ourselves outwardly against others will bring the hollowness of the spiritual wasteland of which the late poet, T.S. Eliot, wrote. In the East the accent is on experience, on one's own experience, not a faith in someone else's, writes the famed expert of myth, Joseph Campbell. "The disciplines (yoga, meditation, fasting, etc.) are ways of attainment of unmistakable experience—ever deeper, ever greater—of one's own identity with whatever one knows as 'divine.' " Western religious experience has too long been handed down as an endowment from those who originally had such enlightenment. What is needed now is to have each individual with such a valid strength behind him. Too many in today's world believe, in Mr. Campbell's own words, "Let me first correct society, then get around to myself . . . but since all societies are evil, sor-

rowful, inequitable . . . and will always be,'' if you want
to help the world you will have to teach yourself how to
live in it.

In analyzing the different so-called ''levels'' of consciousness it will be helpful to consider man's evolution in other
ways than a linear one—that is, instead of a development
from cave man to hunter and villager to city dweller.
Myths of many cultures as well as artifacts which have
survived, point to the possibility that high cultures existed
earlier and a period of backwardness intervened between
then and now. Joseph Campbell suggests from the facts
of mythology that unity was greatly evident in the early
records of man, and that this period was followed by a
split between what he terms the true occult (the understanding of hidden origins, etc.). In this second stage when
divinity in man is suppressed, possession follows. The
following stage (from which we are finally emerging) is
the stage of the hard world of fact, and we are preceding,
as the consciousness revolution is showing, once again
towards unity.

In psychointegration the lowest level of consciousness
is that of jungle or animal survival. At this level life is a
combat, and the highest priority is the survival of the
biological organism. Because life is a combat, killing the
outsider is considered a moral duty. There are, unfortunately,
still communities in the world today which function largely
at this primitive level of consciousness.

The second level is that of sexual gratification and
reproduction. With survival, which was threatened in the
first level, secured, a life in the pleasure of the senses
begins to receive priority. A by-product of this is love
both for one's offspring and one's sexual partner. The
latter relationship is often one of eros, a primarily physical love. Freud helped us understand the problems of development in this level which related to Abraham Maslow's
third need, ''Love, affection, and belongingness,'' a need
which is intensified in a sick society.

The most obvious expression of the third level of consciousness, power, is the ruler of the state, the leader of

any group, the administrator. But even the mother must come to terms with this level in her relations with her children. This level, more than the others tends to stress a relationship with others which makes others objects to be manipulated, what Martin Buber called an I-It relationship. At this level the ego is very strong in its demands for satisfaction. In extreme cases, this level of consciousness is characterized (1) by a willingness to sacrifice personal values for the acquisition of power over others (2) by pleasure in the control of others, their submission to one's will. This level should not be confused with the power of creativity which is released from the Unconscious in higher levels of consciousness.

At the power level of consciousness, the ego can experience the maximum of inflation, which is obvious to anyone who has studied political figures throughout history. At this level the individual's self-esteem is based on his power. Often infant feelings of inferiority begin the compensating drive for superiority.

We wish to caution the reader who may wish to analyze or attempt to catalog himself or others by these various levels. Their usefulness lies in understanding the main energy thrust of the individual's personality and it is often necessary to move among the levels to achieve one's daily roles.

When evolving between the third and fourth levels, the individual passes through the narrow gate of suffering. In Carl Jung's "individuation" process the healthy ego (conscious mind) goes through alternating cycles of inflation, rejection, alienation, and penitence until it is strong enough to resist truly shattering deflation and its accompanying suffering. At this time then, after surviving his suffering, the person can begin to transmute his self-love into love of others. Biological love for a mate or offspring is transmuted into love of mankind, and the person arrives at the fourth level, one of conscious awareness, that of heart and compassion. Jesus was the embodiment of this agape love. Eric Fromm, Abraham Maslow and other humanistic psychologists have written of this level and its needs which lead the individual to become a "self-actualizer."

The fifth level is the search for God. In one's Unconscious, there are emanations from the God archetype whether in the form of Einstein's scientific awareness of the "irreducible mystery of the universe" or the recognition of "ultraconsciousness" (the mystical experience). In their ignorance, those who have not experienced such levels often decide that the entire concept is an empty one. They are often guilty of what the pioneer psychologist, William James, called the "nothing but" fallacy; further levels of consciousness are reduced to "nothing but" one's own less evolved consciousness and, all too often in the West, are disposed of as pathology.

If we go outside of the lab we find that evidence is now available which allows us to say that some men and women have demonstrably achieved higher levels of consciousness. Because of the subtlety of the phenomena, the evidence so far tends not to be laboratory data but interviews and biographical accounts. But if numbers of men and women have given evidence of greater wholeness, why should not all aspire to that condition?

As Abraham Maslow said in *Motivation and Personality,* "Ought a biological species to be judged by its crippled, warped, only partially developed specimens, or by examples that have been over domesticated, caged, and trained?" "The average man," writes Gopi Krishna, in "The True Aim of Yoga" (*Psychic* 1973), "oblivious to his own divine nature and unconscious of his own majesty, lives in permanent doubt because of the limitations of the human brain. He is overwhelmed by uncertainty and sorrow at the thought of death and identifies himself with the body from the first to the last. He does not realize that he has a glorious, unbounded, eternal existence of his own."

The search for wisdom can bring men into the sixth level—in which one's knowledge can be structured to include all meaningful human experience, even its paradoxes. As the teacher—entity Seth says in *Seth Speaks*; the only way

to avoid rigid concepts of right and wrong is through true
compassion and love. These will lead to an understanding
"of the nature of good, and only these qualities will serve
to annihilate the erroneous and distortive concepts of
evil." In arriving at wisdom, one must become aware of
the restrictive nature of hate which narrows down and
shadows experience. One must not even hate "hate." Hate
is powerful if you believe in it, as is evil, and minds
focused upon these destructive elements in human experience must achieve a higher perspective if they are to
reach any valid kind of wisdom. He who hates an evil
merely creates another one, Seth warns.

Guilt also is destructive in the evolution of consciousness. It can lead to a paralysis of will in which the ego
is overawed by the challenge, and may result in cynicism
about the possibility of attaining the higher levels, or even
deny their existence. Those who, for whatever reason,
feel guilt when they become aware of their own unfinished
psychological business should ask themselves, "Does the
artist feel guilt over the part of his creation which is as
yet incomplete?" Not usually. The growth of the psyche
is a slow process of unfolding through which each individual proceeds at his own pace. The object is ultimately
the discovery of the Self (the soul), not becoming normal
or adapting socially, although these things will be the by-
products as one approaches harmony. As the individual
approaches wholeness, he will exhibit increasing freedom
of will—the deterministic influence of environment and biology will fall away.

Patience is a prime requisite for individuation or the
evolution of human consciousness through the seven levels.
It is better to think of a widening and deepening of consciousness, rather than a climbing.

The seventh level, that of full enlightenment, has been
sustained by only a few—Jesus, the Buddha and others.
Few continue long in the physical realm at this level.
One either returns with a peak experience to illuminate
and guide one for the rest of life or leaves the physical
body. Thomas Merton lived only a short while after ex-

periencing Samadhi, its highest level, that is. Many have
come into this level through the traditional mystical experience, which is more recently being called "ultraconsciousness." Awareness at this level leads the individual to great
creativity and, occasionally, to the founding of a new
religion. The individual here experiences a trans-personal
awareness in which the ego identity loses much of its
remaining importance. Individual ego consciousness is
supplanted by cosmic consciousness. "Illumination" explains Gopi Krishna, "represents a transformation of
consciousness, the opening of a new channel of perception
which the deathless and boundless universe is opened to
the vision of the soul." At this level what men call faith
is replaced by knowledge gained through experience. Faith
is superseded by an authentic spiritual consciousness.

At each level the individual's motivation changes as
his life acquires a different meaning. This is not to say
that a conscious search for meaning exists before the
fourth level, heart-compassion. In the early stages the individual may be conscious by the usual definition but his
motivation is largely instinctual and unconscious. His
state of consciousness is *aconscious,* which is to say
that he might be thought of as a kind of sleep-walker,
particularly in respect to objective self-awareness. After
the ego encounters real suffering, (that suffering which
initiates the major crisis of individuation midway in life),
he may then begin his awakening to consciousness in
preparation for ultraconsciousness, should it come.

One of the major problems inherent in the nature of
the human being is the confusion surrounding who we
are. With minds open, like radio receivers, to an influx
from the thought world around us, learning how to distinguish our own inherent mental pattern and that of
surrounding influences is often a tricky problem. While
we are growing in true self-awareness, spiritual teachers
of today suggest that mental bubbles of light protection
be built daily around ourselves, our homes, cars, and
loved ones.

The following case illustrates how strongly negative

urges of the emotions, either from outside the individual, or from her own unconscious contents, created fantasies in the conscious mind which was fed by dream material. In this case the dream material seems not to originate just from a closed circuit in the Unconscious, but from an involvement with other beings of the astral realm. The resulting agony caused years of suffering but happily growth was the eventual outcome.

Betty was the child of an alcoholic mother. She states that while she was inwardly hungry for some kind of guidance, she was never given any as a child. At the age of fourteen, she had a sexual encounter which was followed by sexual desires so profound that a suicide attempt followed the termination of the affair. Like any appetite, sexuality easily builds its own momentum. At this time, however, she decided against further sexual experience and was free from what she calls undue sexual distress for seven years, that is until several years after her marriage. After the age of fifteen, however, she began having a reoccurring dream of a man standing over her, grinning, and trying to smother her.

After the birth of her second child, she became involved in an extra-marital affair with a black man during which the earlier obsession returned. Once again at the end of the affair, the subject felt the urge to kill herself and attempted suicide. A wildness of laughter which was usual for her and increased alcoholic consumption were both part of her downward plunge.

Once before in her life, at the age of four, a car full of teenagers had veered out of control and she was compelled by an unseen force to move swiftly onto the porch, even though she had no conscious fear. Similarly, during this second crisis of her life, as her problems accumulated, she seemed to be rescued. A dramatic incident triggered her growth. A man who had been staying with the family threatened to kill her, and in her own words, "suddenly a feeling of peace came over me—it felt as if particles of light were enveloping me." At once she found the strength to tell the man to leave, which he immediately did.

Soon after this, at the age of twenty-eight, the subject realized that a change had to be made in her values. She was forced to admit that sexual and intellectual development were not enough. It is perhaps merciful that, even at this time, she did not realize that she had been sexually dominated from another realm, her own behavior from puberty on having drawn about her the smothering obsessing entity who appeared in her dreams repeatedly.

Now a debate began as to whether she should move back to the vicinity of her family in the south or return to graduate school. Again, it seemed like help was available outside herself. She was almost forced to return to the family area. Here she began, under our counselling, to read parapsychological and spiritual materials and she found her attention turning to prayer, meditation, and the Bible among other subjects. She asked and received help through prayer, and the reading that she did at that period was so illuminating that, in her own words, it was like coming home.

Harmony is growing steadily in the family and the energy that found expression in sexual excess is being channeled into the service of others. She feels she is beginning to focus at the heart and compassion level.

Earlier we discussed the Unconscious and its marvelous ability to intervene to save the life of the individual. We can see this functioning in a remarkable way in the case of this woman, who twice was given help from outside herself, without expecting or asking for it. The Unconscious, whether pictured as the channel to Divine Mind, the Higher Self or the "Great Man" within, apparently does function without the aid of the conscious mind.

"Experience in analytical psychology," writes Carl Jung in 'The Transcendent Function' (1916) "has amply shown that the conscious and the Unconscious seldom agree as to their contents and their tendencies. This lack of parallelism is not just accidental or purposeless, but is due to the fact that the Unconscious behaves in a compensatory or complementary manner towards the conscious." All elements that are too weak in intensity stay in the Unconscious, Jung found. Consciousness inhibits all incompatiable material with the result that it sinks into the unconscious. In the case of Betty the innate good with which she longed to make contact earlier in life had not yet attained the intensity to break across the threshold of consciousness which separates the unconscious and conscious minds. But the help was there, as it is in each of us, waiting for the time and suitable circumstances to enter the light of consciousness, and at a time when it (and it's moral demands) can be understood. Perhaps man's psychological potential is truly God's manifestation in him.

Jung wrote that the direction and the definiteness of the conscious mind are extremely important acquisitions which humanity has bought at a very heavy price and are achievements which have in their turn, "rendered humanity the highest service." Without them science, technology, and civilization would be impossible, for "they all presupposed the reliable continuity and directedness of the conscious process." But the disadvantage is that the directedness of the conscious mind excludes all the psychic elements that appear to be incompatible with it, and so judgments and goals become one-sided. We call that reasonable which appears to be reasonable to us; therefore the unreasonable is doomed because of its irrationality, Jung felt. But the more we remove ourselves from the Unconscious, the more a "powerful counter-position can build up" and the consequences that follow this, should it break out, can be destructive in many cases. In 1918 Jung, for example, predicted the Nazi horror from this psychological principle.

For Jung, the solution was to get rid of the separation between the conscious mind and the Unconscious. This could not be done by condemning the contents of the Unconscious in a one-sided way, but rather by taking into account the significance of its compensating function. He calls the two modes of consciousness working together the "transcendent function, because it makes the transition from one attitude to another organically possible, without

loss of the unconscious." The Jungian analyst helps bring
the conscious and unconscious functions together to arrive
at a new attitude. The best source of unconscious material
with which any counsellor can work is the material which
comes from dreams.

In the case of Jane we see a perfect example of the
transcendent function, the transition from one attitude to
another being administered through the agency of the Unconscious acting as a channel for Divine Mind. Whether
the powers which save us are from without or immanent
within our own unfolded natures is not the question, although for all practical purposes they are the same thing.
What is important is the integrated individual, man knowing
himself in his true nature as an atom in the body of
divinity, not subjectivity dominated by unruly emotional
states, which blind him to this truth. Man on earth must
gain control of his emotions. Only then will he be free to
carry on his eventual work in the universe.

Jane moved from years of turmoil in the subjective
emotional realm of experience to one in which her objective spiritual nature could reflect and mirror back serenity.
Through dreams, the out-of-body experience, and visions,
her Unconscious carefully and successfully carried her
through. Today she is rapidly growing in spiritual awareness.

She had dreamed of an unhappy marriage since childhood. The subsequent actuality of her landing in the middle
of such a marriage is a cogent example of interior preparation and guidance. She married in her teens without
love when her suitor threatened suicide. She thought that
perhaps she would learn to love this man who was so
ardent in his affections. She was carrying her second child
when her first knowledge of real love hit her like a thunder-
storm. Without any reasonable explanation, the acquain-
tance of a fellow teacher in her neighborhood brought so
strong a sensation of love that it left her shattered emotionally for many months. To make matters worse, the
feeling seemed to be mutual. The man himself, then married, and their families continued to be closely connected

because of the proximity of their houses and occupations. He was no happier than Jane and even his children seemed to love her the most. The years passed with the strength of attraction increasing between them, and one day they both felt it was useless to continue in the lives which were hollow from lack of closeness.

They had planned to meet after school, the first step in leaving their legal mates, their children, and the community. In fact, they were on the way to pick up her belongings when Jane underwent the out-of-body experience that changed the direction of her life. Though she could still see herself seated in the car, she was conscious of a duplicate self that now stood beside the road next to a radiant being in white, with golden-brown hair and reddish-brown beard. She later was thrilled by the description of the clairvoyant Edgar Cayce's description of Christ Jesus—the hair and beard color matched completely.

A mental communication took place in which the thought came through that she was expected to obey the commandments given on earth. She was to have all of the rest some day. At that time she was shown two scenes, one of her joyful, one of her together with the soul-mate beside her in the car. The effect of this communication in one who had no understanding and had never read of an out-of-body experience began the transformation which followed.

The plans were changed. But the unhappiness continued. It was not until she later read of the out-of-body experience that her doubts about her own sanity were put aside.

There was a further suicide attempt, and then, intuitively, a feeling began to emerge that she was about to experience a change. Drawn powerfully to attend some lectures on parapsychology, her excitement became apparent. As details of the immense world outside of the material senses were explained, she relates that it was like someone let her out of a box. Spiritual tutoring began. She began to read avidly. Before she knew it she realized that she had now a spiritual joy which coincided with the

first picture which she was shown in the foregoing experience. It must have been valid after all, she reasoned.

The question of why such suffering should come to a
person who is loving and compassionate by nature was
also explained in a subsequent dream. She dreamed a large
book opened to a "Chapter Eight." On a page, (she
remembers only the first and most important sentence)
was the following message: "true love does not possess."
It was clear that this was a life-lesson she needed to learn.
Due to this dream, an understanding of her personal
suffering began (and the suffering in this life has been so
strong that it moved to tears the astrologer who did her
chart).

A year ago Jane was filled with a new spiritual joy that
surpassed any pleasure that she could imagine, even the
sharing of life with the loved one. But what about the
neglected husband? From the beginning of the marriage
he had been without compassion or sympathy during the
difficult pregnancies and the problems involved in raising
five children. Unconsciously Jane still carried a feeling of
resentment against him. Last March, however, she awoke
one morning, and it was, in her words, "Like I was inside
his head." I understood the agony, the emotional suffering, the loneliness that he had endured, and it completely
destroyed any resentment I had harbored." Now in her
new found objectivity, she can give love serenely to this
one who stood for so long as a barrier to her happiness,
and she has, without doubt, emerged from her life tur-
moils with a heroic nature.

That is what the life royally lived is: an adventure
lived in terms of inner dynamics, the inner dimensions
of your own actions. This is the god-within-man which
will save the world—it is what, by his actions, the hero
shows to the whole world.

Why is it that some will lay down their lives for others,
Joseph Campbell, the well-known mythologist, recently
asked. Why would it occur to any of us to make sac-
rifices, to grow beyond ourselves if it were not for the

god-nature in man that strives to be expressed. That our growth has been long delayed is not the point. What is important is that we are waking at last.

A sense of the urgency of western man's circumstances is well expressed in these words of George Leonard: "Each year brings us closer to the realization that our present way of doing and being cannot last very much longer. If our shift to a new mode of existence is to take place voluntarily before catastrophe strikes, we shall need to get on with the business of converting our energy-economic system from exponential growth to something approaching a steady state, a process that itself will require great amounts of energy. The human brain, the most complex entity in the known universe, has not necessarily evolved merely to aid in the production and consumption of ever more trivial goods and services. Perhaps this complex and marvellous entity can help us turn to other kinds of wealth, non-material wealth, and other kinds of energy, the energy of the Spirit, which burns no fuel, depletes no resources, and creates no pollution." "Reason has served humanity only transient truths; can we now dare to hope that perhaps the mind has far greater capacities?" writes Beulah Bosarge. During the last century, in the biologist's view, there has been no room in the body for the soul, but in the traditional religions of the West, there has been no room for the personal religious experience, a far greater tragedy.

We have been discussing consciousness in this chapter in a framework of levels which correspond to Eastern philosophy. The link between East and West foreseen by the American poet Walt Whitman seems to be emerging. What is so greatly needed in our day is a dynamic, experiential faith which can serve both the individual psychologically and the culture sociologically. As the English parapsychological researcher, Sir Alister Hardy, recently said, "The pragmatic intellectualism of this nation fused with the intuitive Spiritual outlook of the East could provide the power which could evolve men's minds and hearts."

Should the philosophies of the East and the West fuse

and produce evolved minds both singularly and en masse, then man will participate in a new energy source, a new power. Teilhard de Chardin foresaw a humanity which might be the sum of organized persons. Should the day come when the personality is experienced as actually including (and embracing) other people, self-consciousness or self-awareness then truly becomes social consciousness. Inner growth must precede social reform. Only then can come the psychological revolution of the ages—social justice expanded through awareness of the self.

Chapter III
Understanding Consciousness Through Dreams

"Dreams which are not interpreted are like
letters which have not been opened."
                    The Talmud

Throughout history, most cultures of the past have held
a wide range of beliefs about the function of dreams. In
many cultures, dreams were carefully evaluated and were
drawn upon for daily guidance. In other words, dreams
played an important role in the conscious, waking state.
Several centuries ago, at a crucial juncture in the intellectual development of the Western mind, the importance
of dreams began to be lost. As a result the interpretation
of dreams was no longer widely practiced, and dream interpretation became simply a tool of the psychotherapist.

There have been various conceptions of dreams down
through the ages. They have been considered as the real
experiences of disembodied souls which have left the body
during sleep, the result of illness or indigestion, and as
inspired by God or evil spirits. With Freud they began
to be considered as the expressions of our irrational passions. Later, with Carl Jung and Erich Fromm, they become
expressions of our highest and most rational powers. It
would be unwise to consider dreams solely in the light
of one point of view. All of these theories are but facets
of the emerging realization that dreams *do* contain vital
information about consciousness and personality.

51

The breakthroughs in dream study began in the early fifties when Eugene Aserinsky pinpointed a phase of sleep during which rapid eye movement (REM) was observed and from which dream remembrance was more frequent. For the first time a behavioral index was available to indicate when people were dreaming. In the Western world, until 1953, when this discovery and others to which it led were announced, it was believed that a dream was a random instantaneous experience and that a dreamless night was beneficial to health. Then Professor Nathaniel Kleitman of the University of Chicago Department of Physiology, world expert on sleep, reported a series of experiments on the fluttering eye movement of sleeping infants which his student, Eugene Aserinsky, had observed. Using an EEG machine to record the electrical activity of the brain, Aserinsky and Kleitman observed four distinct patterns of brain waves spanning the entire sleep period. They called the lightest sleep Stage 1, a stage which corresponds most closely to the kind of record obtained when one is awake. Stage 4 is a very deep stage of sleep, closely related to a coma. It was found that during seven or eight hours of sleep, there were four or five periods of return from the deeper stages of sleep back to Stage 1, each involving about 90 minutes each. At first about five minutes were spent in Stage 1, then the sleeper descended rapidly through 2, 3, and 4 where he remained approximately thirty minutes. On the second cycle, he spent much less time in Stage 4 (approximately 12%) and much more of the time in Stage 1 (the light stage), so toward the end of the sleep period, in a 90-minute cycle of descent and ascent, the subject was spending 25% of his time in the first and second stages. These were the stages of the vivid and memorable dreams.

Although patterns of sleep vary slightly between individuals, the cyclic nature of sleep has held true in thousands of subjects involved in sleep experiments.

Turning over preceded or followed State 1, the sleeper being very difficult to awake in this period of the rapid eye movement (REM) sleep. When there was a change of body posture, it ended one REM dream and began another. The Chicago researchers noticed that the eyes moved in unison, the sleeper completely still as if watching a play. Dr. Ann Faraday describes the REM sleep as a period of "heightened cerebral, ocular, and autonomic excitement" (*Dream Power,* Dr. Ann Faraday, 1972).

In the non-REM, or NREM, stage of sleep, paradoxically the deep stage, dream recall was only 7% and the sleeper could be awakened easily. NREM dreams were discovered to be shorter, less active, more plausible, more concerned with current problems and more thought-like; while the REM dreams involved the sleeper dramatically, emotionally, and more deeply in general. These dreams usually consisted of more than one episode and subjects reported that they were visually intense, so much so that the recall of REM dreams was found to be around 80%

Perhaps the most important fact emerging from the study of REM sleep is its importance to psychological well-being. In the mid-fifties, Dr. Charles Fisher and Dr. William Dement, working at Mount Sinai Hospital in New York, woke patients in a dream study experiment for five nights in a row at the first sign of REM sleep. At the end of this period, though the subjects had averaged six hours total sleep, they complained of psychological discomfort, suffered anxiety, and began to eat more than usual. When allowed to sleep undisturbed, they spent 60% more time in REM sleep, as if making up for the lost dreams. Like reactions occurred with cats and rabbits. After being awakened or deprived of REM sleep for 26 days, the animals went immediately into the REM period and spent 60% more time in it than usual. In every experiment, whether with man or animal, an "orgy of compensatory REM time followed deprivation." It is a unique state, believed by some investigators to be "subserved by different brain mechanisms" (*The New World of Dreams,* Woods and Greenhouse, 1974). Obviously, we are meant to dream and to experience the vivid and dramatic REM sleep.

During the dream studies a difference between the recallers and the nonrecallers became evident. The difference between the two types is apparently a matter of the psychology of their personalities. Nonrecallers showed more eye movement during the REM period and it was discovered that these movements resulted from looking away from an object instead of looking at it. The bulk of evidence suggested that "nonrecallers are decidedly reluctant to remember their dreams, just as they tend to avoid or deny unpleasant experiences and anxieties in everyday life," writes Dr. Ann Faraday. Theirs was a deliberate repression. Nonrecalling patients of psychoanalysts fail even to remember the disguise of their dreams. Recallers on the other hand are shown to be more willing to confront their emotional disturbances, which indicates their interest in the inner, subjective side of life, in growth and self-knowledge.

It was not long ago, when the 18th century fostered the Age of Reason, that dreams lost the importance that they had held for thousands of years in practically every land. In *The Forgotten Language,* Erich Fromm reminds us that, in the "enlightened" view of that period, which has persisted almost to the present, dreams were considered the "senseless and insignificant manifestation of our minds, at best mental reflexes of bodily sensations experienced during sleep." A change of attitude began very slowly when Sigmund Freud's book *The Interpretation of Dreams* was published in November of 1899. Over the following eight years only 600 copies were sold and Freud remarked bitterly, "My psychiatric colleagues do not seem to have taken any trouble to overcome the initial suspicions which my new conception of the dream produced in them." In this book Freud analyzed the dreams recounted to him by patients as well as a number of his own. While recognition of the importance of the work was slow in coming, nineteenth-century thinkers such as Ralph Waldo Emerson helped bolster the importance of the dream state for mankind. In *Lectures and Biographical Sketches,* Emerson said, "Sleep takes off the costume of circumstances, arms us with the terrible freedom, so that every will rushes to a deed. A skillful man reads his dreams for his self-knowledge. . . ."

Freud considered the irrational in dreams to be the result of irrational passions and desires rooted in childhood (i.e., the child forced underground in the adult) and, though the recent discoveries in dream research clearly show the limits of this point of view, Freud must be given credit for his conceptualization of the subconscious, as well as for his account of man as a psychological entity which operates as a self-regulating system. The three sub-systems of his total psychological system are described as the Preconscious, the Conscious and the Unconscious, the latter being considered by Freud as primarily "instinctual" energy. Such energy, in his opinion, tended toward the achievement of states of gratification, and he considered wish-fulfillment as *the* motive for dream activity.

Freud was more suspicious of the subconscious than was his young colleague, Carl G. Jung. Freud believed that emotional experience held in the subconscious necessarily needed to be prevented by repression from gaining access to the conscious mind and thus disrupting the tenor of one's life. Freud's hypothesis, that the dream's function was "to guard against disruption by anxiety-provoking unconscious impulses, is now under sharp attack and defense as a result of the host of new findings regarding the physiology of sleeping and dreaming," writes Dr. Jay Shurley in "Changing Concepts of Dreaming" (*Currents in Psychoanalysis*).

Dr. Shurley explains that the electrophysiological study of dreaming has become "the prototype of a whole new and exciting strategy in the study of consciousness, which complements and extends the introspective and psychoanalytic method." He feels that it is now possible to unravel the evolutionary history of human consciousness.

What Dr. Shurley is saying has been put another way by Erich Fromm: "If we downgrade dreams as expressions of the irrational side of our natures, valuable insights into our affairs, present and future are lost." The growing view of today is that the function of dreams is not only to solve problems, but to awaken man to his full stature as a person.

In the Adlerian theory the material of dreams was thought to consist of problems from conscious experience, not as in Freud's belief, "screens for something else." David Foulkes in "How Is the Dream Formed, Another Look At Freud and Adler" (*The New World of Dreams*) feels that it is apparent from the Dement and Kleitman data that both Freud and Adler misjudged the conditions under which dreaming occurs. Most adult dreamers spent approximately 20% of their time in REM sleep with little variation, regardless of whether or not they had personal problems. There was little evidence of libido or hostility in the pre-REM thought from which dreams are thought to develop. The NREM contents, after much dream study, do not show personal anxiety or insecurity, but seem unconnected with the psychological concerns of the dreamer.

Freud's follower and one-time colleague, Carl Jung, disagreed radically about dreams. Jung saw them not only pointing to the future, but showing the goals and aims of the dreamer and it is the Jungian viewpoint that modern research tends to bear out. This was one of the reasons for Jung's belief in the wisdom of the Unconscious. For him it was potentially superior, a basic religious phenomenon through which a voice or source transcending man could speak. One is reminded of the writer Job who states:

> God speaks first in one way,
> and then another, but not one notices.
> He speaks by dreams, and visions
> that come in the night
> when slumber comes on mankind.

> (Job 33:14)

Readers who doubt the possibility of detailed and patient guiding from the Unconscious would do well to check the records of one hundred and fifty-four dreams submitted by a Southern woman to the clairvoyant Edgar Cayce, for interpretation over a four year period. With his careful analysis of the case in his book *Edgar Cayce On Dreams* (1974), Dr. Harmon Bro brings us a fantastic picture: dreams which show how to evaluate basic drives, problem solving dreams which either give a solution to a problem or awaken the dreamer to a state of mind in which he can reach a solution, dreams which show the time to carry new responsibilities, or to develop more mature natures, and cycles of dreams aimed at developing new qualities in the dreamer such as patience, balance, altruism, humor, reflectiveness, and piety. Francis saw that her dreams were working to solve both outward problems as well as to quicken her inner potential. Dr. Bro writes, "As Cayce saw her dreams, nearly half of them contained reference or challenge to her life-orientation, to her ultimate values and commitments. . ."

Using the analogy of a ship for the body, Bro described the equipment aboard which must be operated successfully, some to serve the passengers, some to serve the other equipment. Likewise does the Unconscious operate through dreams to guide the sleeper in the proper maintenance of the equipment of the body so that it might operate smoothly in its internal functioning and its relationship to other people. The following dreams illustrate the point. Bro presents a dream which Francis had after a miscarriage, a dream of having some trouble which prevented her from having a baby and the necessity for correction through a slight operation. On the operating table, given the anaesthetic, she feels herself losing consciousness, the doctor's fingers growing lighter in touch. She is conscious of herself losing consciousness and of its consummation. Then she comes to, the operation having finished, and the nurse says she can have a baby very soon.

Cayce saw this dream as very positive—the word consummation referring "not simply to childbirth but to sexual release which she could choose pleasantly and safely, giving to her "body-conscious" that experience of the condition through which (one) passes to attain childbirth.

At the time of Francis' pregnancy, her sister-in-law dreamed that Francis had a new flexible diamond bracelet. On the same night Francis herself dreamed that she had bands on her fingers which opened into flexible diamond bracelets to the elbow. She stayed home from her classes to enjoy the wonderful jewelry. The bands signified marital union, opening into arm bracelets—the opening development of her marriage with the coming child.

In another dream, after Francis had committed herself to a rather unwise diet eliminating all sugar and starch, she dreamed of having an ache in her side and of going out into a rain of starch to ease the ache. Here again the body was problem-solving through a dream. Cayce explains that the lack of starch was causing fermentation in organs on the right side of her body.

Dreams relating to the physical, including the body's need for exercise, a balanced diet, play, hard work, healthy elimination, medical care, sexual orgasms, and quiet meditation, all these crowded "the stage of dreams" in Francis' case. In the Cayce view, there are, in effect, only three levels in dreaming: the levels of body, mind, and spirit. The body itself, Cayce learned, can initiate "dreams which call for physiological help through the assistance of the unconscious."

Such a case is that of a woman meditator who had been several years on a meatless diet. During a period of extreme menstrual flow, she had the following dream. She was driving her car when a policeman pulled her over to the side. Unaware of doing anything wrong, she questioned him. "You're driving too close to the liver," he explained. She began crying and said that she just wanted to get to the hospital. The following morning after the dream, a friend dropping by to visit and remarked upon how pale the woman looked. Then the dream flashed through her mind and its meaning became clear. She was badly in need of iron. She began supplementing her diet with it that day and the change in her health was immediate.

Here we see what Dr. Bro calls the dreamer's subconscious, "his hidden structures, habits, controls, mechanisms, complexes, formulas"—using his own "memory images and figures of speech to get things done." Author Claude Bristol, with other analyzers of the unconscious mind, feels that one of its important functions is the intuitive understanding of bodily needs, which it maintains and preserves without the aid of the conscious mind (i.e., the autonomic body processes).

Let us now look for a moment at the way in which the Unconscious seems to have ability beyond that of the conscious mind. A graduate math student was involved in a difficult course which was primarily based on self-study. Her frustrations mounted with her inability to do the work properly and she relates that most of the problems were not mastered but "massacred." One evening after a particularly frustrating experience of using her procedure for three hours, she was unable to come up with the correct answer to a problem although the method she had used to work it had been correct. In despair she went to sleep and soon found herself sitting up in bed saying aloud, "I've lost a one (1) in the denominator, in the divisor . . ." It seemed that she fell immediately back to sleep, but the next morning the words reoccurred to her. "When I re-approached the problem, I had only to look at a small portion of the problem, in which I had divided one polynomial equation into a second one of higher degree. And there, before me," she writes, "was my error! In multiplying the quotient times the divisor (the denominator, synonymously) I had, indeed, dropped a *one*."

After this experience the student felt it necessary to back away and analyze her whole method of approach to the course, for it was clear that her unconscious was working far better than her conscious mind. She then began to strive for a more relaxed method of approach. During a very long oral exam, she reports that she answered the questions with such exactness that it surprised her teacher. He not only lauded her on her performance, but admitted himself to be jealous that his student understood the latter half of the course better than he.

Cayce spoke repeatedly of the Unconscious and its use of its own ESP to get hold of practical matters. But in his opinion, a higher source of help, "the superconscious," was available. The forces which Cayce called the Creative Forces could provide the individual with "boundless" information and very necessary guidance.

Current investigators such as David Cohen seem to be in agreement with the Cayce view. Writing in *Psychology Today*, Cohen observes that dreams are taking their place as valuable inner messages, and clear pictures of ourselves and our relationships to others, even inspiration for creativity. A dream of Mr. Charles G. Abbott, now retired Secretary of the Smithsonian Institution, who has been working in the field of astrophysics for more than seventy years, is a case in point. In 1965 he awoke one night to see exactly how a solar burner for turning sunlight into electricity could be built on a commercial scale. The dream which he wrote out the next morning became U.S. Patent No. 3,376,165. At last report he was working on his 175th scientific paper and considered dreaming an important aid.

One is reminded of the help which Thomas Edison received from his hours of dream-reverie for his numerous inventions. Einstein's theory of relativity which took three weeks to write down was revealed to him in a dream. Great men of the past, Descartes, Goethe, Tolstoy, Mozart, Schumann and Wagner drew insights into nature and their art from their dreams. A Nobel Prize winner in chemistry, Maria Meyer, saw in a flash the constituents of the atomic nucleus.

Not only symbols but images carry the meaning of dreams. In a twelve-page essay in his own hand, Einstein explains the importance of the images which appeared in his mind, conveying his first theory of 1907. He wrote, ''Mental pictures seem to be the essential feature in productive thought before there is any connection with logical construction in words or other kinds of signs which can be communicated to others.''

All dreamers of telepathic and pre-cognitive dreams realize the importance of the mental image, often an exact duplication of a future event. A middle-aged woman recalls seeing a monk's face in a dream while still in her teens. Thirty years later, after a divorce and the accompanying problems of raising children alone, the man of her dream appeared in her life and they were married. The monk's attire expressed an early wish of his to be a monk. This dream is powerful in that it suggests a future fulfillment conveyed to the dreamer at a very early age, though not understood. It is estimated that at least 10% of the population have precognitive dreams but are unaware of them as such.

As early as 1928 an English psychical researcher, G.N.M. Tryell in a book *Science and Psychical Phenomena* cites a dream of "a curious kind." Dreamer Dudley Ealker dreamed of being over a signal-box over a railway-line he had never seen before. He saw an excursion train full of people returning from some function. Inexplicably, he felt as though the train were doomed. Hovering in the air, he followed the express as it slowed to round a loop and saw, to his horror, another small train approaching from the other side of the same line. They met with terrible impact, and walking beside the wreck later, he saw in his dream, bodies, mostly women's and girls,' a man dead on an over-turned couch; all the details that appeared in the newspaper the following morning coincided with his dream. Because Mr. Walker had given a detailed account of the dream to his boss and his mother before the news was known, this case could be documented. Cases of such dreams, which number in the thousands, show possible telepathy at work.

We have the next three dreams from our own dream experiences. After fifteen years of wondering if the U.S. involvement in South Korea had been worthwhile the following dream occurred in the spring of 1974. An old Korean woman appeared on a hot, dusty Korean road and said, "You won't be sorry you came out here." This dream shows the multiple function of dreams. It was helpful to the personality because it explained something of importance to the dreamer and it was also clairvoyant for the following day the newspaper headlines were: "Two Koreas Seek Unity."

A young lady barely known to us was involved in an unusual dream. On a visit, in the dream, we noticed that two women who seemed to be attendants sat on either side of her on the couch. They would not let her go outside into the garden. She was holding back tears but was too weak to protest. Five days after this dream, it was learned that, on the night of the dream, she had been hospitalized as a result of using a poisonous spray. Also, for 24 hours before the doctor discovered the fact of the poisoning, the nurses had treated their hallucinating patient as if she had been emotionally ill.

A dream of a coming head-on collision in which one of us, then planning a trip to Texas with his parents, would be involved, was so vivid that plans were changed. He withdrew from the trip though the rest of the party continued. In the exact location as in the dream, south of Waco, Texas, an oncoming car, whose driver had fallen asleep at the wheel, ran head-on into the relatives' car, putting them in the hospital for several months. This dream occurred many years ago and subsequently has, as will be the case with anyone who has a proven dream of precognition, interested us in the mechanism at work in dreams.

An unusual dream of precognition occurred five times to another young woman dreamer before it happened in reality. In the dream the dreamer, a nurse, was visiting her next-door neighbors when the husband slumped out of his chair with a heart attack. Isolated in the country and beyond immediate aid, her only recourse was to give him mouth-to-mouth resuscitation. In each dream the events were the same, he always slumping to the floor, she at his side giving aid. When the event at last happened, she states that she was so prepared by the foregoing dreams that she was at his side almost immediately. Her efforts, however, quick as they were, were not sufficient to save him. Perhaps the dream alerting her to the need of very quick action alleviated any self-blame that she might have felt if she had been unprepared.

Another young nurse experienced a warning dream a day before the actual experience which it foreshadowed. On a routine delivery case, in the dream, she was asked by the doctor to prepare and administer a drug to a patient in labor. The child was stillborn and there were complaints against her for possibly giving the wrong amount of the drug. The following day a delivery case of the identical doctor in the dream came up. As in the dream, she was asked to prepare and administer the medication. Remembering the dream, she asked an L.V.N. to watch her prepare and give the medicine. The child was stillborn but because of the care she had taken for protection, no blame was assigned to her.

Harold Michaels, administrator of the Alameda Hospital in Alameda, California, had a vivid dream of a large jet airliner crashing into an apartment complex killing ten people and injuring forty-one. Because of the dream, he began thinking of how the hospital would handle such an emergency and began a disaster drill and monthly meetings to sharpen up procedures. Nine months later a Navy jet crashed into an apartment complex five blocks away from the hospital, as was in the dream. In Mr. Michaels' own words, "Before the victims even arrived at the hospital, we were completely ready for them. We had six surgical teams scrubbed and in their gowns, ready to go within minutes of the crash. Over fifty doctors showed up within ten minutes, and seventy-seven employees in addition to those already on duty. We could have taken care of three or four times as many victims as we did, if the need had arisen."

Cayce called such guidance the "creative currents of the Divine itself, moving through human affairs like some Great unseen Gulf Stream." One might reach in his dreams beyond his own limits through his own "superconscious" to tune in on these Universal Forces.

It is interesting to compare Freud and Jung on the matter of the telepathic in dreams. Freud was initially cautious about telepathy, but was interested in tracing it in the dreams of his patients. In a 1921 paper called "Dreams and Telepathy" Freud said, "It is an incontestable fact that sleep creates favorable conditions for telepathy." In a later piece, "Dreams and the Occult," he conjectured that telepathy might be:

the original archaic method by which individuals understood one another, and which has been pushed into the background in the course of phylogenetic (evolutionary) development by the better method of communication by means of a sign apprehended by the sense organs. But older methods may have persisted in the background, and may still manifest themselves under certain conditions.

"The transfer of thoughts, the possibility of sensing past or future cannot be merely accidental," he said at the age of eighty-two, yet he maintained for most of his life a great mistrust of clairvoyant prophecies and dreams, not even attempting to document various dreams which took place before events.

Possibly because he himself had had prophetic dreams (it is said that Freud had none), Carl Jung was more open to them. Concerning awareness of future events, he wrote, "They're evidently not synchronous but are synchronistic since they are experienced as psychic images in the present, as though the objective already existed." In such cases there seems to be

an *a priori*, causally inexplicable knowledge of a situation which is at the time unknowable. Synchronicity therefore consists of two factors: A) An unconscious image comes into consciousness either directly (i.e., literally) or indirectly (symbolized or suggested) in the form of a dream, idea, or premonition. B) An objective situation coincides with this content. . . . How does the unconscious image arise, and how the coincidence?

Perhaps it was such questions as these which spurred the organization of a medical section of the American Society for Psychical Research in 1948 to report on paranormal findings "in light of psychiatry." Included in this group were Dr. Jule Eisenbud, Dr. Montague Ullman and Dr. Jan Ehrenwald. Dr. Eisenbud had contributed greatly to dream telepathy and dreams took predominance in the discussion because of their importance as a psychoanalytical tool. Dr. Ehrenwald, author of *Telepathy and Medical Psychology*, with a rich background in neurology and psychiatry, noted the accuracy with which patients could tune in on the private lives of their analysts through dreams. He reports thirteen points of correspondence between one of his patient's "dream apartment" and his own living room, including French doors, a large terrace, and a lack of a maid's room and second bathroom. After a similar type of dream reported by another patient, Dr. Ehrenwald set up an experimental condition to see if a new patient could recognize his dream location. The results are so intriguing that we give the story in full.

On the Sunday preceding the dream, Dr. Ehrenwald walked with his wife and daughter in their neighborhood to have a close look at what they called their private Champs Elysees: a wooded wasteland off the outlying parts of Queens Boulevard. "Huge mounds of earth cut through the hill terrain," Ehrenwald records, "gave an impression of a dam being built. The mounds of earth dug up by the bulldozer had a sandy color. A big water tower structure dominated the view from the 'dam.' "

That night the patient had the following dream. He was walking with two women and a five-year-old boy along a straight canal with dams of freshly plowed earth on both sides. He tried to phone somebody, the connection was cut, but he put the wires back together and reestablished the connection. He walked around a large square (Ehrenwald walked a square mile) and saw something like the Eiffel Tower and the Champs Elysees at a distance. The land was like sand dunes and the terrain went up and down.

The five-year-old boy apparently stood for the dreamer in the dream, for he had been used to walks with his family as a boy. The water tower in waking life corresponded nicely with the Eiffel Tower, and, of course, the image of the Champs Elysees stunned everyone. The re-establishing connecting wires represented, Ehrenwald felt, making telepathic connections. The parallels of sandy color, rolling terrain was another hit.

Dr. Jule Eisenbud has contributed to the understanding of paranormal dreaming; his book *Psi and Psychoanalysis*

demonstrates among other things that dream telepathy can
be used to hurry a patient's recovery. He reports that many
patients experience a sense of awe when they see the meaningful coincidences which the Unconscious can provide. Jung
called this sense of awe "numinousity," from the Latin
"numen," divine will. As Drs. Montague Ullman and
Stanley Krippner put it in their book *Dream Telepathy*
(1973), "The emotional impact of this 'divine will' burns
the experience into (his) consciousness and the patient
takes the dream messages profoundly to heart."

> When patients who have never met have intermeshing dreams
> on different nights and these dreams become meaningful
> only when discussed with their common point of contact, the
> psychiatrist, one begins to wonder just who might be sending
> telepathic messages to whom . . . . One might speculate the
> human relationship may be guided and influenced by some
> fundamental underlying force that occasionally surfaces into
> consciousness as psi events, particularly during emotionally-
> laden situations.

Ullman and Krippner also say, "Perhaps, during these
times, a collective consciousness is formed between the individuals involved."

Whatever the mechanism, the value of such dreams to
the individual is often considerable. Before the death of
her mother, Francis, her husband and mother, all had
dreams preparing them for the actual event. She dreamed
that she and her sister were on the bed with their mother
in the hospital and were crying, "Don't leave us." The
mother who was unconscious awoke and started to talk
very loud and unlike herself.

Her husband dreamed of Francis crying, symbolically
emptying herself to take in greater spiritual understanding.
The mother, during the time in the hospital, dreamed
that she saw all of her children and associates and they
all appeared dead.

Cayce explained that this dream showed the sick mother
that her unconscious was viewing from a "superconscious

perspective how far each person in the dream fully comprehended the relations between earthly and post-death life.'' They were seen as dead because they would have to go through ''a death of false attitudes and convictions, if they were correctly to understand what she was going through.''

When the mother had a temporary recovery, Francis had a dream which previewed it, but later the same night she had dreamed of a man dressed in pure white who pulled her mother into the light. She later dreamed that her mother was well and was to be married. There was much merry-making, but her mother would be operated on again and would die, as was the case. She would, however, according to the interpretation, awaken in another plane of her existence which was the cause for the merry-making.

On the night of her mother's death, Francis dreamed of her mother's close friend who had died three weeks earlier. She states, ''The impression of her talking to me was very pronounced and for a while I did not see her figure, yet I felt that she was with Mother at the hospital, as Mother changed from this earthly consciousness to the other. . . she said to me, 'Your mother is as happy as ever.' ''

Such experiences make claims from paranormal sources such as the following from *The Seth Material* relevant to the topic we are discussing. Seth explains, ''The characteristics of consciousness are the same whether you are in a body or outside of one,'' and that when such a possibility sinks home, all of us will begin to see the importance of raising, healing, and unifying our individual consciousness for it is our home, our soul awareness and it creates for us the environmental situations in which we find ourselves, as well as the patterns for our future. ''Your consciousness is telepathic and clairvoyant. . . . In sleep you may be far more conscious than you are now, but simply using abilities of consciousness that you do not accept as real or valid in waking life. You therefore shut them out of your conscious experience—Consciousness, yours and mine, is independent of both time and space. And after death you are simply aware of the greater powers of consciousness that exist within you all the time." The main thing is for our consciousness not to over identify with the body.

Anyone further interested in following contemporary research on telepathy in dreams, should read the account of work being done at the Dream Laboratory of the Brooklyn Maimonides Medical Center in *Dream Telepathy* by Drs. Montague Ullman and Stanley Krippner. Even Freud himself would have been impressed by a dreamer hitting six out of eight targets during sleep as a telepathic receiver, at odds of 10,000 to 1.

Here is yet another case from our files which illustrates the collective working of consciousness—even after physical death. A sixteen-year-old girl dreamed of meeting a high-school friend in the middle of a street. He took her hand and said, "Come, I have a friend who wants to talk to you." She describes walking down the street together and seeing at the end of the street only "vast, white light." She saw waiting inside the light a mutual high school friend who had been killed in an automobile accident several weeks earlier. He was perfectly whole and normal and waited inside the white light for her to come. As she approached, she noticed that he was extremely upset, concerned about his mother. She went to him and put her arms around him, as a mother does a child. He stayed with his head on her breast and when later looking up, seemed whole again and had a very peaceful and beautiful smile.

She states that she began to cry for happiness. He pushed her to the street where the other friend was waiting. He, too, had tears in his eyes. They turned and proceeded back toward the town. It should be noted that the girl who experienced this dream is quite psychic and has healing abilities as well as a basic spiritual orientation.

The whole question of the activities of consciousness when the sleeping body is at rest needs to be looked at in a new or rather a very old light. "Certain of the Greenlanders," writes Sir Edward Tylor in *The New World of Dreams* (1974), "consider that the soul quits the body in the night and goes out hunting, dancing and visiting; their dreams, which are frequent and lively, having brought them to this opinion." Among the Indians of North America, we hear of the dreamer's soul leaving its body and wandering in quest of things which are attractive to it. This view is also held by the New Zealanders who believe the dreaming soul leaves the body and goes even to the region of the dead for conversation with its friends.

Most of us know someone who has dreamed of meeting departed loved ones and experiencing a "visit" from them in which they warn or give suggestions. The Zulu and the North American Indians believe that they may be visited in a dream by an ancestor who comes to warn of danger or to take them to visit their distant people. The sleeping hours of the Negroes of South Guinea are "characterized by almost as much intercourse with the dead as their waking are with the living," Sir Tylor writes. "Among the North American Indians, and especially the Algonquin tribes, accounts are not unusual of men whose spirits, traveling in dreams or in hallucinations of extreme illness to the land of the dead, have returned to re-animate their bodies, and tell what they have seen." Curiously enough science through the filming of the energy field—perhaps a reflection of consciousness energy—is showing that it is the returning "spirit" body which does re-animate the body which has lain unconscious during sleep. The energy-field disappears even under hypnosis.

Mostly, in the legends about the dreaming state, the dreamer's soul is thought to leave the body behind in states of sleep, death, coma, or ecstasy. One is reminded of the experience of Paul who describes having visited the third heaven, whether in the body or out of the body, he knew not. Visions of saints and mystics throughout history have repeatedly suggested the validity of experiences outside of the physical realm of activity. One of the most amazing cases on file is that of the "lady in blue," a Spanish nun who, for eight years, apparently bi-located in sleep to work and teach the Indians of America in the West.

In *Seth Spreaks* by Jane Roberts, the teaching entity Seth explains: "If you do not understand that in periods of sleep your consciousness actually *does* leave your body, then what I have said will be meaningless . . . . Your consciousness does return at night at times to check upon the physical mechanisms, and the simple consciousness of atom and cell—the body consciousness—is always with the body, so it is not vacant. But the largely creative portions of the self do leave the body, and for large periods of time when you sleep." Seth goes on to explain that there are peaks of consciousness during which one should rest, not "jack up" themselves with stimulants. Making a natural use of these rhythms would increase concentration and we will discuss this further in the next chapter on meditation. However, it is important to note that long periods of waking consciousness build up chemicals in the blood that must be discharged in sleep; long periods of sleep are then necessary to counteract the long waking periods and these are detrimental to the body, for the body's work is increased and must perform continuously to bring about the purifications which would ideally be taken care of in shorter periods of rest. This also creates a sense of duality, Seth explains, and a mistrust of one part of the self toward the other. Not only is creativity lost by such a procedure of long waking and sleeping periods, but the symbolism of dreams is also lost, along with a flexibility of consciousness, and strengthening of the entire personality. Seth asserts that the body's chemical processes, particularly the adrenal glands, proceed more efficiently with shorter periods of alternation between active and resting states. We are not aware of current medical research on this point but it has perhaps been studied.

Again Seth says, "Consciousness does not refresh itself in sleep. It is merely turned in another direction." We are spirits now whose consciousnesses may be turned off and on. It helps in this connection to think of ourselves in terms of energy receivers, of varying wattage like light bulbs. A healthy body and mind gives off more light or energy, as the Kirlian process shows. A balanced mental and emotional state, as well as proper diet, meditation, and outdoor exercise, all contribute to tuning ourselves up to the best performance of which we are capable. By balancing ourselves, we will affect not only our own lives and those of our friends, but the natural surroundings as well. The healers, Ambrose and Olga Worrall, in a plant experiment with Dr. Robert Miller in Georgia in 1967, changed the rate of growth from 0.00625 inches an hour to 0.0525 inches per hour for a rate increase of 830% (*The Probability of The Impossible,* Dr. Thelma Moss, 1974). This natural link between all living things was discussed in Chapter One with Cleve Backster's work.

We have discussed the literal, symbolic, problem-solving, creative, telepathic and pre-cognitive dream. Dreams which stimulate the growth of consciousness may be the area of greatest contemporary interest.

The young bride Francis had dreams which previewed the death of attachment to the physical diversions and the growing capacity for thought and creativity. She dreamed on the same night, first that she had died, and secondly that someone was wearing a dress which she copied and wore. The left sleeve of the dress was very tight and they told her in the dream that that was the way it should be. Then she said, "Make me two just like this."

"Cayce described her 'putting on of apparel' as evidence of the awakening of her subconscious to put on its new potentials," writes Dr. Bro. But he warned that ordering two dresses showed a bit of pride.

As her unconscious awakened she began to have dreams which pinpointed the health problems of her loved ones, making it possible for her to help them. She was able to contact in her dreams her discarnate parents who warned of her sister's potential suicide. Only the timing of the dream and many hours of counseling saved the sister from the actual act of taking her life.

In the long and demanding process of the growth of consciousness, anyone desiring help should certainly begin both to log his own dreams, and to unravel his own individual use of symbols. Otherwise this significant source of wisdom will be lost. Much of the dream guidance which we will receive will be, as was the case for Francis, a correction of attitudes and emotions, of habitual and harmful ways of reacting.

A middle-aged woman who had moved many times during her husband's military career, finally became settled for a number of years in a community when she was threatened by another move. She dreamed of being in a boat and going over the same channel over which she had traveled before, around a boat house where the boat struck something and began to sink. Meditating on this dream herself, she came to understand that its message warned against self-pity, an attitude which she had carried with her and which was capable of sinking the boat, or vehicle in which the Self traveled.

A younger woman was preoccupied and worried about the part Jesus played in religion and had been unable to accept Him personally as the only way to God. She dreamed of a gold Virgin Mary medallion, oval in shape, which seemed to have Mary's face on it, but which became a spray of white light with Jesus on the cross. As she watched the body became a skeleton and the dreamer was drawn in to see the head and eye sockets and teeth. She awoke in horror.

The interpretation of the dream suggested that it symbolized certain aspects of her own nature: (1) a horror of death, (2) a horror of any illumination which would disfigure or change her, and (3) a distrust of emotion. She readily agreed with the validity of the dream as instruction. Also she was helped to see that she had already learned "the way to God" through service, love, humility—the very things that Jesus had taught, and that through continued service she could overcome the negative emotional trends and gain rule over her own life.

A young nurse dreamed of trying to heal a little black

girl. She took her upstairs to a higher room where healing could take place. In the dream there was also a baby pig which symbolized the young woman's lower nature which tended to be stubborn. She was unable to coax the little pig up the stairs. The young nurse's handling of her emotions had often been immature and in the dream the mind was working in symbols to clothe what she needed to know. The little black girl symbolized the dreamer's own shadow self, which needed to be healed.

The newcomer to the study of dreams may be troubled by their contradictory elements, particularly because we have been urging the reader to take dream guidance seriously. As Erich Fromm reminds us, we are "not only less reasonable and less decent in our dreams, but also more intelligent, wise and capable of better judgment when we are asleep than when we are awake." One is also reminded of Jung's Shadow (the personification of our negative traits) and the Self (the personification of our higher nature).

In "A Life Study In the Evolution of Consciousness" (1975), Mr. David Cammack relates a series of dreams which show a gradual awakening in a young woman dreamer. The following is what he calls the touchstone dream. She recalls:

There was a cat sitting beside us and an ashtray between us. I started to spin the ashtray and it started going around very rapidly and picking up speed. As it was spinning faster and faster, we were sitting watching it, and I started to drift away with the spinning. Then I realized I was lifting off the ground and floating closer toward the ceiling. As I came closer to the ceiling I became frightened of what might happen when I hit it. I realized I did not have control . . . I noticed the door and forced myself toward it. I realized it had a brilliant blue aura around it. I was hoping the door was going to be my escape from the ceiling. But as I put my hand to the knob to open it, I became very frightened of what might happen if I went outside. I thought I might drift away and not come back. So again I forced myself away from the door . . . as I came near the ceiling I turned and faced downward to the floor. Then I started to descend.

As I was coming down, in amazement I saw my body lying on the floor. And as I came close it opened up like a box and I entered. Then it closed behind me.

The young wife was told that this out-of-body experience signified her hesitancy to advance spiritually at that time, for she was afraid to pass through the door surrounded by the blue aura. "Due to her fear of the unknown regions of higher levels of consciousness, twelve months passed before she had another significant dream," Mr. Cammack writes. After a period of suffering due to her father's ailing health and a trip abroad to see him, she had returned to the States and experienced this pre-cognitive dream:

One night I met my father in a dream. My body was floating away in the skies and who should I meet floating toward me but my Dad. I said, 'What are you doing here?' He answered, 'I came to tell you not to worry about saying good-bye. I am very happy where I am.' He then disappeared.

Five days later she received a letter which stated that her father had died during the same evening on which she had met him in her dream. Cammack reports that being out of her body did not disturb her this time, emotionally or intelectually. But "it was some months later before she decided to become actively involved in her own spiritual evolution."

Recognizing the need for self-discipline, the young woman began to keep a log of her dreams. She began a morning rest period of hypnogogic sleep or meditation. She would record and later discuss any dreams that seemed to have particular significance.

During the next consecutive three months, she reported dreams of communication with her father, of healing, of counseling in the spiritual realm, of precognition and most important to her own development, of the symbolic unity of the ego and the Self.

"One of (her) earliest significant dreams included the

promise of the future development of powers of spiritual healing." She dreamed of getting a message between waking and sleeping, "You will help them and heal them." She dreamed that a friend was getting married and at first she was not going to get her a gift, but then decided that she would. At the wedding party, there was a table full of gifts. Her gift was outside of the door, a plaque with words she does not remember. Everyone thought it a special gift; to her it was very simple.

Cammack feels her hesitancy to give the gift was significant of her long delay in pursuing her spiritual evolution and that not remembering the words indicated that she needed to refine her spiritual perceptions.

Some time later a dream occurred which seems to relate to the message of healing received earlier. That afternoon a friend had received a threatening call in answer to an item she was advertising in a local paper. Her husband was out of town for the weekend and the caller had her address. The young woman and her husband decided to stay with the woman that night, and took the bedroom she usually occupied. The young woman dreamed that a man was beside the bed with a weapon in his hand with which he was going to attack her. She looked at him and said: "Just one minute. Before you do that I want to talk to you."

"With that I was rather startled and woke up wondering if he was really there," she relates. "I looked around and listened. I saw and heard nothing so I went back to sleep. Just then, as I was going back to sleep, there was the man again. He was kneeling by the bedside listening to me. I was telling him about people who love as well as those who hate, and that there was good and bad, not all evil. I talked to him for a good while, and then realized he had tears in his eyes. He was sorry for his bad thoughts and actions. There was no more. My sleep that night was a bit broken and restless."

One of her most recent perceptions had been the realization of the symbolic unity of the ego and the Self, according to Cammack. "Due to her highly developed sensitivity

and poorly developed emotional sophistication, she has
trouble dealing with negativity.'' he writes. In one dream
she was attempting to escape through death but was warned
that she must develop strength to deal with her life conditions. In a second dream of the same night, the ego and
the Self functioned in harmony. Rain, negativity, threatened
a journey she was making. It was too late to return for an
umbrella. She and her traveling companion had to perform
in harmony in a large tavern (representing the area where
she lives) before continuing their journey, an indication of
the necessity for the development of harmony both between
her emotional development and her level of sensitivity,
Cammack feels. At the end of the journey she was to meet
her father, whose presence symbolized the culmination of
spiritual advancement.

Due to the volume of help given by the Unconscious
through her dreams, she has begun to understand the importance of suffering and hard work, as well as the purpose
and pattern of the evolution of consciousness within her
own life. She now also has faith in her ability to advance
her consciousness.

For six months Marilyn, age 22, had been living with a
boy whose criticisms had brought her to a situational paranoia which seemed to challenge her very identity. The
subject is a nurse; paranoia is her own description. Subsequent events make her psychological symptoms seem
situational and temporary if indeed it was paranoia. A few
weeks before the dreams here discussed, her instinct for
survival had caused her to leave her boy friend and go to
another state. Even away and on her own she carried a
heavy psychological burden. She hesitated during several
days of great emotional stress to discuss her problems
with another person. Finally, though she had remembered
no dreams for a period of five months, her Unconscious
provided her with the following two dreams on the same
night.

I'm in a women's prison camp. I go outside and am given
a stone by a friend of mine, a woman . . . who happens to

be in a relationship with a man . . . The significant thing about that to me is that they are both very spiritual people and in a beautiful relationship as I see it. It has been prolonged over two years and they will probably be married. The woman brings me that stone and on it are the directions as to how to get out of the prison camp. She hands me the stone and hurries off, telling me not to let anyone catch me with the stone because it would be really incriminating. The stone has been sent from her romantic partner. I go back in the prison camp. The female warden gets really upset because she thinks that I have escaped. I have been hiding under the bed covers. I come out and everything's cool. Then I escape. The directions as to how to get out were written on the stone.''

The hiding place of the stone was explicitly linked to sexual activity. After her escape, she was being driven in a car by the boy with whom she had been in a relationship; the car was driven ''up a mountain curving road'' as she ''begged him not to speed. If anytime he goes the speed limit,'' he should go slow *now*. [This last dream incident indicates that, for her psyche, restraint is *now* crucial]. Even retelling the following dream was a powerful emotional experience for the subject.

In this dream I met the devil. It begins in a large institutional type of setting. I'm with this guy that I'm having this relationship with and all these problems with. We are told by some unknown person that there is a fire and we should get out. [Fire of lust or purification?] So we have a warning so that we can get out before the mad panic. Pretty soon everybody is trying to get out; the panic has started and I'm in the middle of the institution and I feel very alone even though there are people all around me because I see that the devil is materializing in front of me as a dark shadow form and I see that he has chosen me out of the whole crowd to confront. He comes closer and closer and as [it was a powerful experience reliving this dream as she told it] he comes closer and closer I am really terrorized, I am just overcome by fear, I'm having all kinds of adrenalin rush [?] I'm scared to death. I clap my hands together and the only thing I can think to do is just praying out loud as loud as I possibly can. My eyes are closed, I'm shaking, I'm trembling. I remember praying the Lord's Prayer and the devil kept coming closer and closer and I realized that as I was denying him by affirming God, he seemed to be losing power. I seemed to be gaining power over the situation. And as he lost power I could tell that he wanted to test me as a last resort. He was really going to catch me and so I just prayed harder and screamed. I was *really* overcome by fear. And about this time, the test was that he plucked my eyeballs out, he stuck a hot dagger in my solar plexus and I overcame the pain of the whole experience by the praying I was doing and affirming God's existence and denying the devil. It ended about right there but I sort of mastered the situation.

After retelling and discussing these dreams she agreed that, despite their heavy contents, they were "very comforting." She said, "I realized that they were making me confront problems in myself that I had denied." She also experienced "great relief" as the contents were assimilated. She recognized that the Unconscious had presented her with an issue which had to be confronted. The issue, of course, was her own sexuality and its relationship to her identity crisis. She had experienced what she described as a "breakdown of her self-image due to his hypercritical nature." This she felt led to much irrational fear which she considers her first true objectivity, including the first objective decision of her life. These dreams were, therefore, a "turning point in her life."

Prior to these dreams, she had, she felt, gotten her life lopsided; even her usual practices of prayer and meditation were ignored. In terms of individuation, these guidance dreams clearly pointed the way to growth: out of the women's prison, or the limitation of an exclusively sexual identity. Apparently sex was almost the only basis for communication between these as yet not fully formed personalities. The larger context is then a major crisis of individuation, during which the ego, threatened by growth and the ensuing new role, experiences great fear and an identity crisis. For this young woman the new role was a life in which her psyche's energies were primarily focussed at the sexual level of consciousness. From her description of her previous development, it was a growth period which compensated for a previous imbalance which had denied her sexuality. These dreams made clear to her that, once again, growth required compensation.

No study of consciousness growth furthered by dreams would be complete without looking at recent experiments with dream incubation. This ritual, used by modern psychologists for guidance and healing goes back at least as far as the ancient Egyptians who spoke in reverence of "a divine dream from the gods." There are many classical examples of kings and pharaohs throughout the ancient world receiving divinely-inspired messages through dreams. Daniel attempted and succeeded in incubating a dream which would interpret a dream which King Nebuchadnezzar had forgotten. But perhaps the classic example of dream incubation used on a wide scale by the populace was in the dream temple of the Greek god Asklepios. A person with organic or psychological problems would simply go to sleep in the temple and Asklepios would appear in his dream either to prescribe treatment, diagnose, or do a symbolic operation. Testimonies of the prescriptions and healings exist today. Dream incubation, writes psychologist Dr. Henry Reed, is "the ritual of going to sleep in a sacred place in anticipation of receiving a helpful dream from a divine benefactor . . . (and it) illustrates the viability of the ritual seeking guidance and conflict resolution from dreams."

The American Indians used dream incubation for healing and other quests; fasting youths would remain in the wilderness until a dream revealed by one from the spirit world showed them their own particular gifts and supernatural aids which they might use in the future.

Dr. Reed, who uses modern psychotherapeutic procedures and principles, describes his work in an article "Dream Incubation" (*A.R.E. Journal,* March, 1972). Some patients involved with dream incubation had no dream recall and were eliminated from the study, Dr. Reed explains. Others who had dreams showing conflict and who had a desire to understand their problems were involved in the study and all successfully incubated dreams.

In this procedure, a person picks a date one to three days in the future. He chooses his personal symbols, the purpose of the incubation, and his "sacred place" which should include feelings of safety, comfort, and nurturance, a place where he feels centered and at peace. The revered benefactor can be someone he admires, dreams about, fantasizes about, trusts or considers wise, loving, or as having healing abilities. We see these ideas operative today in personal retreats, churches, shrines, gurus, and doctors, Dr. Reed feels.

After getting as clear an image as possible of the situation or conflict which he needs to resolve, the dreamer must examine the ways in which he is benefiting from such conflict, and decide honestly if he is willing to let go of the resistance in order to be able to accept genuine change. He must see how accomplishing his purpose will put him in greater harmony with life and his highest ideal, Dr. Reed explains, and also how others will benefit as the dreamer fulfills his purpose. If he decides that he is ready to make use of the possibilities offered, a 24-hour symbolic cleansing such as fasting from food or certain attitudes is necessary. Before the sleep period in his experiment, Dr. Reed played forty minutes of classical and then emotional music to "discharge emotional material," and help the subjects relinquish control of their stream of consciousness as well as all attempts to deal with the problem themselves. After building trust in the autonomous processes, there followed what Reed calls an "externalization of a psychological fact," that is "a natural inner process of self-regulation, healing, or transformation." How delighted Carl Jung would be to see contemporary acceptance of his trust in the Unconscious.

The meanings of the dreams which followed were allowed to develop over a period of time, rather than being forced to fit a particular interpretation. Some dreams of course had meanings which were immediately perceived. A man who had been frustrated in his work as a result of cynicism about himself which had been fostered by his father, dreamed of receiving the "positive emotional support" he needed from his father and woke up crying. He thereafter had a fresh capacity for his work and subsequent meaningful dialogues with his father.

A fourteen-year-old boy involved with drugs, first dreamed of a voyage in which water-logged creatures were longing for dry land. In his incubated dream he was walking down a long and dusty road, which was choking him (representing what was expected of him in school and society). He climbed a tree, spotted an axe, and proceeded to cut his own path which was cool and refreshing. After this dream he was able to initiate his own projects at school, and get away from drugs. He later dreamed an even more promising dream of finding a jewel-studded sword.

"I suspect that the value of the dreams obtained from incubation comes from some synthetic mixture of the experience of the dream itself, elaborations given to the dream image, meanings perceived through the medium of the dream and the test piloting of these meanings into daily life," Dr. Reed writes.

Individual study groups around the country are also working with dream incubation successfully, and it is most promising to see a serious interest in recalling and using dream material. There was danger in not doing so, according to Edgar Cayce, for the psyche might be forced "to get in touch with itself by crisis or illness." Dreamers might also "lose their capacity for guidance and growth by dreams" through escapism, self-love, hypochondria (*Edgar Cayce On Dreams*, Dr. Harmon Bro). One woman reported that she deliberately kept herself from dreaming because she feared a dream portending her husband's death, which seems unwise in the light of recent findings.

Cayce advised that those using the strong energies of the Unconscious through dreams should at the same time try to live balanced lives, otherwise the energies could be destructive at night. Though dreams are self-regulatory, when one upsets his body, mind or soul balance, he upsets the "regulatory function of dreams." Neither should one let his fascination with dreams over-ride the need for action in the physical.

We see dreams then as a very valid way of opening a gateway into consciousness.

"Consciousness is a way of perceiving the various dimensions of reality," says the entity Seth in *Seth Speaks*. "The physical senses allow you to perceive the three-dimensional world and yet by their very nature they can inhibit the perception of other equally valid dimensions. Most of you identify with your daily physically oriented self. You would not think of identifying with one portion of your body and ignoring all other parts, and yet you are doing the same thing when you imagine that the egotistical self carries the burden of your identity . . . ."

Seth goes on to explain that because our conscious mind, as we think of it, is not aware of these activities, we do not identify with this inner portion of ourselves. Instead we identify with the part of us which thinks it knows what it is doing. "But this seemingly unconscious portion of yourself is far more knowledgeable, and upon its smooth functioning your entire physical existence depends." This seemingly unconscious within us, Seth calls the "inner ego," for it directs inner activities and correlates information that is received through other channels than the physical senses. He calls it an "inner perceiver of reality . . . " which looks into "subjective dimensions that are literally infinite . . . . " It is from these subjective dimensions that "all objective realities flow."

Before we can lift a finger or flicker an eyelid "unbelievable (inner) activities take place . . . . All communication takes place long before a word is spoken," for this portion of our identity is natively clairvoyant and telepathic. . . . "This 'inner ego' and 'outer ego' work together, one enabling us to manipulate in the world that we know, and the other bringing us "those delicate inner perceptions without which physical existence could not be maintained."

The Unconscious is the meeting place between the inner and outer egos, but there are no real divisions to the Self.

Again he warns, ''The ego is a jealous god, and it wants its interests served. It does not want to admit the reality of any dimensions except those within which it feels comfortable and can understand. It was meant to be an aide but it has been allowed to become a tyrant. Even so, it is much more resilient and eager to learn than it is generally supposed.

''If you have a limited conception of the nature of reality, then your ego will do its best to keep you in the small enclosed area of your accepted reality. If, on the other hand, your intuitions and creative instincts are allowed freedom, then they communicate some knowledge of greater dimensions to this portion of your personality.''

We are reminded of the well-advertised phrase from *Jonathan Livingston Seagull*, ''perfection has no limits,'' when Seth says that the self has no limits; and yet it is this fact that science is beginning to show us. There are no limits to our potentials but we can adopt artificial ones, if we choose, through ignorance. Identifying with our outer egos alone will cut us off from abilities which are part of us, and by so doing, we do not change the facts, but only limit our intuitions, creative instincts and freedom to achieve. These are vast dimensions of ourselves that we are gaining access to through dreams, meditation, as well as through scientific investigation; these are the parts of ourselves, well removed from the conscious mind, which carry our real ideals and commitments, our best self. Let us explore in the next chapter further ways of reaching them.

Chapter IV
Meditation: Your Inner Riches

"Go not outside, return into thyself:
Truth dwells in the inward man."
St. Augustine

Thus far we have sought to show how the centuries-old restraints which man has imposed upon himself are beginning to break down under the combined weight of scientific investigation and spiritual claims. As the faint glimmer of the truth of our innate potential, from which we had turned aside (either from past failure or some ancient over-lay of guilt), eventually lights the human mind, a new pathway will open. No way, either past or present, seems more fitted to the needs of today *and* is more tested by time than the ancient art of meditation. Meditators have known for years what researchers are now claiming about consciousness: it is the primary avenue to all inner experience, and the basis of all inner knowing, perceiving and states of being.

In the past, religious conceptions of ourselves and our world were taken to a large degree on faith; in the new age that is beginning to change. It now seems essential, if we are to survive, that all men learn to experience for themselves the truths on which faith was based.

E. Rousselle, writing in "Spiritual Guidance in Contemporary Taoism" (*Papers From the Eranos Yearbook*, ed. J. Campbell, 1960), says, "It is of fundamental importance that man should actually experience—and not merely note intellectually—the opposite pole in himself, his unconscious

84

and his vital force." All of our much vaunted scientific knowledge," writes Anthony Campbell (*Seven States Of Consciousness*, 1974), "is without a foundation unless we have some focus, some 'still point of the turning world' to which everything can be related."

Transpersonal psychology is now claiming that a capacity for self-transcendence, ecstasy, the peak experience, spiritual discipline and universal values can be studied empirically (John W. White, "The Consciousness Revolution," *Saturday Review*, Feb. 1975). Such study is now being done with subjects like Transcendental Meditation and kundalini. In "Transcendental Meditation Goes Public" writer Dan Goleman describes the physiological benefits with both TM initiates' and doctors' reports.

Basically all meditative techniques are anti-stress techniques, so it is not surprising to find a range of physiological improvements occurring in meditators. Lower heart rates and blood pressure, changes in brain waves and skin resistance, as well as lessening dependence on drugs and alcohol have been established as benefits. Some meditators were found to be breathing only four times a minute with no over-compensatory breathing, no build-up of carbon dioxide and a normal level of oxygen remaining in the blood. Earlier Maharishi Mahesh Yogi, who is responsible for making TM known in our time, had predicted that scientific research would demonstrate reduction in body metabolism through meditation. The conclusions of such research have just reached the public in the last few years.

All of the physical benefits of meditation, however, are by-products of the mental and spiritual experience with which meditation is concerned: reaching the inner Self. Knowledge of the whole process once existed, but we have so hemmed in, locked up and cemented the intuitive parts of ourselves, that the wisdom recorded by antiquity may be our only way of finding it.

So we begin by looking at how the great mystics of many religions described God, as being manifested both in us and apart from us in the absoluteness of the Godhead. "He is my self within the heart, smaller than a corn of

rice, smaller than a corn of barley, smaller than a mustard
seed, smaller than a canary seed or the kernel of the canary
seed. He also is myself within the heart, greater than the
heaven, greater than all these worlds.'' (Chandogya
Upanishad). But though the manifestations of God are one
in essence, they are as different as the inner and the outer
man. The purpose of meditation is to still the outer man
long enough so that contact can be made with the inner.
''As the agitated sea of consciousness becomes smooth, the
eternal can mirror itself clearly in the perishable . . . [and we
become aware that] all things are eternally related at
heart . . . . They are *one*: in *Being*, no matter how
variedly we encounter them in forms of manifestation.''
(from K.O. Schmidt's *Laotse's Book Of Life*, 1975).

In this connection, it is relevant to note that science is
moving from a picture of the atom it derived from New-
tonian astronomy, a mechanical system of rotating masses,
to concepts such as ripples, waves, or an undefined movement of energy. Erwin Schrödinger, one of the brilliant
physicists at the University of Vienna, is the discoverer
of wave mechanics. In his book, *Mind and Matter*, we
read, ''The over-all number of minds is just one,'' in which
terms he is describing a religion which ''disinterested scientific research has brought to the fore.'' Particles of photons
and electrons lose their individuality when they become part
of the wave motion. How similar this idea is to the ancient
''all things are eternally related at heart . . . they are one.''
In Lawrence LeShan's book, *The Medium, the Mystic, and
the Physicist* (1974) statements of theoretical physicists are
often identical in substance with those of modern mystics.
These two seemingly divergent viewpoints are beginning to
describe the same underlying essence of creation.

The chasm between science and religion created by Victorian science is, then, being bridged by theoretical physics:
''Occult physics'' is remarkably similar in concept to that
of modern physics, explains Dr. Elmer Green of the Menninger Foundation in Kansas. ''Namely, there is one primary form of energy from which everything else is
constructed.'' As the ancient wisdom and scientific theories

converge, the more sophisticated and intellectual among us
are offered a viable path of liberation. We can begin to
be receptors of the One energy and to experience oneness
both with the Absolute and the innermost core of the Self.

The two cultures, East and West, represent a split from
wholeness, a polarization, according to Ralph Metzner
Maps of Consciousness (1971). When comparing the roles
of East and West to the Chinese Yin and Yang energy,
Metzner says that the creative role of Brahma (a creator
whose role is considered finished) seems to exemplify more
of the yielding "yin" or feminine energy, i.e., "the power of
the Mother principle, the valley spirit of the Taoists, the
shakti power of the Hindus, the all containing void of the
Japanese Buddhists," while the Western culture plays a
"yang" or masculine energy role, exhibiting the aggressive
patriarchal tendencies of the God Jehovah, seeking to conquer the forces of nature. Mr. Metzner feels, as do we, that
a planetary synthesis is now called for, one in which we
learn the Eastern "magnetic receptivity and openness to
higher forces" and the East learns the use of "dynamic
active creativity in harnessing and adapting the forces" of
nature. Since Western seekers have to "search for the missing
half of their lives in the Orient," it is appropriate that, in
attempting to suggest the many facets of meditation, we look
to the East. In so doing, we are in no way suggesting that
the enlightened states discussed are widely prevalent in
Eastern populations.

Anagarika Govinda, German Tibetan Buddhist, described meditation as "the only way to overcome the ego-
complex, the illusions of separativeness, which no amount of
preaching or moral exhortation will achieve. . . . To
give up the smaller for the bigger (the ego pursuits for the
mystical union) is not felt as a sacrifice but as a joyous
release from oppression and narrowness." *(Foundations
of Tibetan Mysticism,* 1969).

Many Western mystics such as the poet Tennyson have
experienced and written about the state beyond the ego.
"I have frequently had quite up from boyhood, when I
have been quite alone (an experience when) individuality

itself seemed to dissolve and fade away into boundless being, and this not a confused state but the clearest of the clear, the surest of the sure, utterly beyond words—where death was an almost laughable impossibility—the loss of personality (if so it were) seeming no extinction but the only true life.'' It is this flash of spiritual understanding of the depths within one's consciousness which meditation can foster.

"When a man is satisfied in the Self alone and has completely cast out all desires from the mind, then he is said to be of steady wisdom,'' says the ancient *Bhagavad Gita;* when one has purifed the mind, mastered the ego and become a ruler of the senses, only then can he realize "his Self as the Self of all beings.'' Oneness is described in other ancient scriptures also. In Zen Buddhism it is called "satori,'' a sudden merging with nature, this merging being the only event that makes the inner life complete. Yoga also seeks to achieve the state of unity or oneness with God, according to Gopi Krishna ("The True Aim of Yoga,'' *Psychic*, January-February, 1973). The yogi uses postures, breathing and other disciplines to achieve this union; the Sufi attempts it in his whirling dance; the Christian in prayer. It is, writes John W. White, "a time-honored technique—probably humanity's oldest spiritual discipline—for helping people to release their potential for expanded consciousness and fuller living.''

At the outset it should be understood that meditation is not, as some may suppose, a merely subjective escape from the world and human involvement. Quite the contrary, it is a discipline in which the body and mind are attuned to spirit so that it can manifest a complete personality in the world. Society is thus enriched. Let us begin with the mind.

"All that we are is the result of what we have thought,'' taught the Buddha. Both Carl Jung and Edgar Cayce describe the fourth dimension as the idea realm. The events that come into being in our three-dimensional world are shaped by the way in which the One energy is channeled through our minds. Thus our minds mediate between that which is pure energy and the physical world. A suggestive

metaphor has been offered by Dr. Herbert Puryear and
Mark Thurston in *Meditation and the Mind of Man* (1975).
Think of a movie being projected. The light shining through
the film is the One energy—the film is the hue our individual
minds, memories, and experiences give, and the results
which are projected on to the movie screen and into our
world are the facts of our lives. "What we see as our
material world is the result of mental processes which have
taken place before that time," they write. "What appears
as form," wrote Lama Govinda, "does thus belong es-
sentially to the past, and is therefore felt as alien by those
who have developed spiritually beyond it." As an idea in
the mind of an architect is transferred first to the blue-
print, then to the workman, and then into the physical
structure of the building we see, so do our thoughts and
desires "create a vibrational pattern" which manifests in
the material world, explain Puryear and Thurston. We
have already shown this concept being demonstrated by
science in chapter one, with the mind's control of matter
and health. Our wills determine how we shall choose to
use these mental functions.

"Only thought is real," say the Hindus, and only through
the mind can the divine be known. By repeated and con-
scientious meditation, one learns to modify his thought
patterns so that what is actualized in his life becomes
more ideal. The meditator eventually learns to live under
the guidance of the higher aspects of his being, the Self.
No matter what his present limitations, with this technique
he can break the shackles of heredity, environment and all
other limiting factors. This is possible because of the neuro-
physiological changes which occur with meditation.

The astounding claims by Eastern meditators and current university research into the physiology of meditation
were summarized recently by John W. White in "The Goal
of Meditation," *Psychic*, (August, 1975). We already know
of ascetics in India who can sit upright in rigid postures
twenty-four hours a day, who can suspend their breathing
for days to be placed in hermetically-sealed chambers for
weeks without suffocation, and who can momentarily stop

the circulation of their blood (this latter we have personally witnessed). White relates findings from the beginning
of this decade. Yogic meditators were found to have more
alpha brainwave activity (a lower frequency) than subjects
at rest; they did not notice loud noises, flashing lights, and
stimuli which normally would take the brain back to the
more active beta range. Consequently they were described
as having no "alpha blocking," being able to hold one
focus until all inner and outer distractions faded. Zen meditators practicing zazen had similar reactions, decreased
heart rate and breathing, less oxygen consumption, the
physiological changes noted earlier. However, because Zen
philosophy stresses being aware of each moment without
intellectualizing about it, the Zen group momentarily reacted
to the loud stimulus. It was also noted that this group had
developed empathy and made excellent counsellors because of being able to relate to others.

Transcendental meditators showed the slow body metabolism which accompanies alpha and low theta brain
waves, which is possibly the level of inspiration, creativity,
and genius. At the University of Texas researchers found
that 20 minutes of TM improved the reaction time of meditators over their pre-meditation scores. Non-meditators
did worse after 20 minutes of ordinary rest. TM meditators
studied at the University of Kansas were found to be generally happier and more relaxed and to have increased
their grades, possibly even their I.Q.'s significantly over
non-meditating students.

"Historically, the goal of meditation has been a transformation of the whole person," writes John W. White.
"Throughout history, teachers of meditation and spiritual
masters have emphasized 'right living' to support one's
meditation. By that they mean a healthy diet; an honest
means of income; an association with virtuous and sym-
pathetic people; truthful speech; kindness and humility in
relations with others; a social conscience; giving up egotistical desire for power, fame, prestige, wealth, psychic
powers, and so forth." However, psychiatrists, such as Dr.
Arthur Deikman, who feel that the importance of medita-

tion lies merely in "changing a person's orientation toward living," are overlooking the crucial mental and neurological changes that occur in the brain and nervous system of the disciplined meditator. Let us look more closely at these changes.

According to TM initiate Anthony Campbell, "Meditation consists in appreciating thought at subtler and subtler levels, until eventually the subtlest level is 'transformed' and the experiencer is left alone with nothing to experience; this is the state of pure awareness . . . . Going deeper within the mind means moving in the direction of increasing 'subtlety' while movement in the opposite direction, toward the surface, is toward increasing grossness."

In explaining the transition from body to mind to pure awareness, Campbell uses the analogy on the physical level of the molecule which is subtler than the crystal, the atom which is subtler than the molecule, the subatomic particles which are subtler than the atom. So on the mental scale, there are similar levels of thought, though they are not usually appreciated consciously. These are thought not concerned with meaning; "it is the quality and not the content of the thought that matters."

During each meditation period several "dives" occur, and the mind alternates between superficial and deeper levels of thought, going frequently beyond to deeper levels of awareness, "and at each step reinforcement occurs, for as the 'depth of mind' between the attention and its goal becomes less, the bliss of pure awareness becomes more and more like a light shining through the fog." The inherent tendency of all minds, TM claims, is to search for happiness and for the "inherently blissful nature of the innermost Self." Because in meditation one continues reaching ever more beautiful levels of thought, the process reinforces itself. No meditator of more than beginning status ever willingly gives up his meditation periods.

"Every dive is followed by a return to the surface," continues Campbell, and during each dive "the attention necessarily traverses the full depth of the mind. In this way

one becomes increasingly familiar with the subtler regions
. . . .'' (*Seven States Of Consciousness,* 1974).

Roland Fischer of the Maryland Psychiatric Research
Center has attempted to chart the various areas of ''inner
space,'' thereby making for a better understanding of states
of consciousness. Fischer's model of ''The Cartography of
Ecstatic and Meditative States'' (Figure 1) was presented
first in *Science* (1971). Fischer describes his chart of inner
space as ''a metaphor for the revolving states of an experiential theatre.'' In his concept all knowledge is innate—
various types of knowledge are tapped, depending on the
degree of arousal. Pathological states occur only when an
individual ''gets stuck in a particular state or role.'' Although the language is new, the basic premise is an ancient
one. In comparison, psychointegration, the philosophy of
personality to be discussed more fully in the final chapter,
describes the state of consciousness of the three levels as
''aconsciousness,'' that of the fourth through sixth, ''consciousness'' and that of the seventh, ''ultraconsciousness.''
As these ascending states become operational in sequence,
the individual becomes aware of ever larger horizons of
knowledge. By contrast, Fischer's model omits the idea of
a lifetime of evolution. Of course, ultraconsciousness is
usually a temporary state which adds to one's understanding of the cosmos, then passes. The lower levels are associated with the aconscious state due to the dominance of
the ego. To some degree the individual will spiral up and
down in these states, depending upon circumstances (Fischer
would say he ''revolves'').

Knowledge from a dream or meditative state can be recaptured when one is in that state again. The new cartography shows a continuum from extreme arousal to extreme
relaxation and the serenity of the samadhi experience. The
ecstatic states are normal with given levels of arousal.

We can see the importance of mind as the vehicle
through which awareness comes, and this accounts for the
importance laid upon mental discipline in almost every
system of meditation (TM is one of the few that believes in
leaving the mind open to let it expand). Meditation has

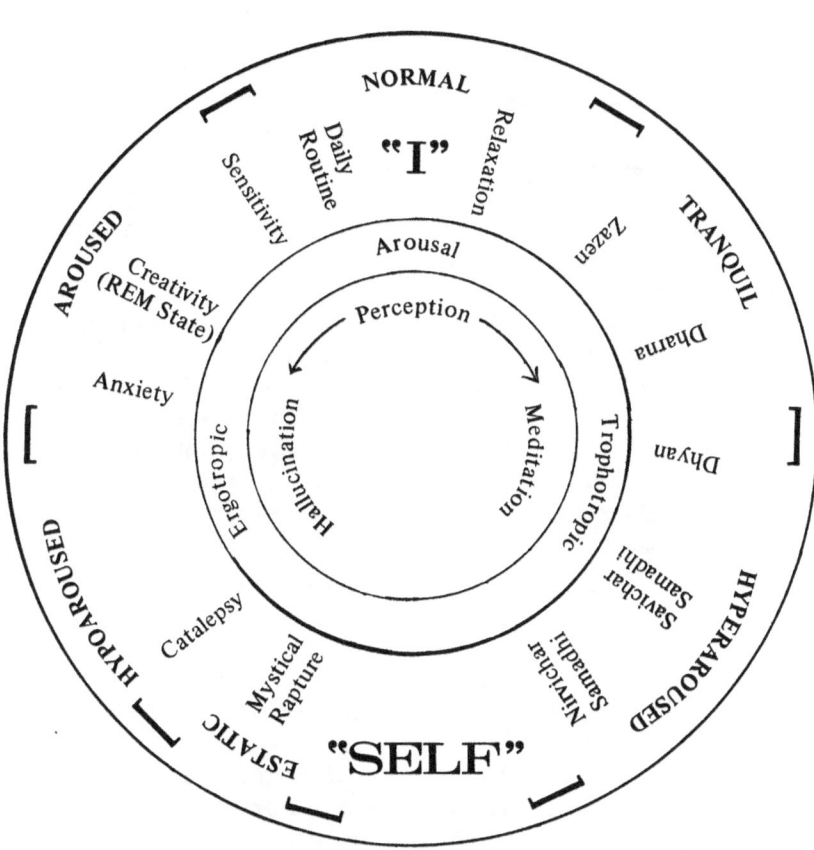

Figure I

been defined as "sustained reflection," "controlled still-
ness." Eastern schools stress a mild form of concentration,
on a candle flame, a mandala, or any device which will
still the outer sense and free the mind for higher insight.
Almost every religious system has a form of mandala from
stained glass rosetta windows to the sand paintings of the
North American Indians. By entering the mandala mentally,
i.e., moving from its outer circumference into the center then
through it, one can reach his own center. Even mandalas
of modern art forms facilitate the transcendence of ordinary
consciousness. By observing, then dissolving through this
visual symbol of the world, the Self, and wholeness; one
can learn the processes of creating and dissolving forms
and images in one's consciousness.

Hindus and Buddhists hold in the mind the thousand
petalled lotus, the Islams the crescent moon, the Jews the
Star of David, the Christians the mystic rose. The Krishna
Consciousness Society chants. Many groups use the mental
repetition of a sound such as "om," a word, phrase, verse
form or religious text. An approach for the Western meditator is suggested by Bradford Smith with the following
eight points:

(1) develop a thought and let it grow
(2) think of your weaknesses and how to strengthen
    them
(3) reflect on beautiful places you've been
(4) see how a problem helps one grow toward
    divinity
(5) look at a friend with love and apartness and
    try to see how you relate to him or mankind
(6) see how life might grow richer and fuller in the
    future
(7) send love and praises to the divine realms
(8) see self inwardly and outwardly

Of the Buddhist scriptures which deal with meditation,
Dhyana is the practice of mind-control by which one stops
thinking and seeks to realize Truth in its essence. "Stopping
is an entrance into the wonderful silence and peacefulness

of potentiality, while realizing is an entrance into the riches of intuition and transcendental intelligence,'' says Grand Master Chic-chi of Tien-tai.

These riches of intuition can be very dramatically experienced if one is involved with creative imagination. In *Gateways to Light* (1974), Flower Newhouse suggests, if you use this form, that you write down the mental and spiritual observations which come, because the random thoughts will have a sequence. ''We are constantly surrounded and penetrated by higher suggestions and encouragements,'' she writes. You wait in a positive expectancy of receiving, and while of all forms of meditation this is the most difficult, it is our experience that dependable mental guidance, a heightened awareness for solving daily problems, and a flowering of artistic abilities can be achieved. ''Creative remembrances requires a high state of receptivity and teachableness.''

Roland Fischer's chart of meditative states gives us an idea of what is happening in creative imagination—knowledge from a given state can be recaptured when one is in that state again. Ideas that come in meditation should be looked at without fear, for as Bradford Smith reminds us, meditation is a gyroscrope that keeps us in balance, with deeper awareness, fuller response and wiser decisions, *(Meditation: the Inward Art,* 1963). It can be used as a vehicle for self-conquest. Smith suggests that we learn to look at ourselves objectively in meditation, as if we were someone else and, having mastered that, learn to look at others as if they were ourselves. ''You meditate just as you play a violin, or make love or write a poem. . .'' he writes, ''out of a desire to merge self with all, out of faith that what you feel in yourself will find a response in others, out of hope that there is indeed a bridge from the human to the divine.''

According to the Cayce material, setting a spiritual ideal is one of the most important experiences one can have in the material world because a re-orientation and re-direction of energy can occur. Yet Edgar Cayce warned against trying to achieve the infinite state before one had done what he could to attune and purify body and mind—it would be like trying to reach "the mountain top without having traversed the foot." So in meditation we work with problems in our characters, in our reactions and habits, and as they are worked out we can open up to the "universal-spiritual qualities."

We have already discussed how repeated meditation involves the mind in increasingly higher and more subtle kinds of energy, but these can affect and benefit us more fully when the body is purified and attuned. Because the body can adversely affect one's mental outlook and spiritual thrust, all forms of meditation stress some kind of physical discipline, whether it be fasting, breathing exercises, postures, bathing, abstaining from meats, coffee, sugar and other stimulants. (Studies now show that the surprising growth of hyperactivity in children can be related to the increase of sugar in the diet.) In time many meditators voluntarily undertake such disciplines themselves because of the increased subtlety a purified system can experience. In ancient China, as in other lands such as Egypt and Greece, physical health was the attainment of every "realized" man who wanted tranquility of heart and mind. Opinions varied as to man's worth and potential, but all of the philosophic schools in China seem to have agreed on the importance of the physical. "There was no school of thought, alchemy, medicine which did not include physical culture as a basic necessity for health and spirituality," writes Robert Cheng in "Tai Chi Chuan." Man's mental, physical and emotional natures were considered a single entity. Even today visitors to the People's Republic report that Tai Chi exercises are done daily in the streets by the old and young alike.

In this connection it will help if we remember that the ancients were believed to be able to see the human "aura," the electrical components of "bodies" which we discussed in Chapter One; these sheaths are not of separate layers but penetrating forms of energy, believed to relate to the mind, the emotions, the health of the physical body itself. If we

LAMAR UNIVERSITY
KIRLIAN PHOTOGRAPHS

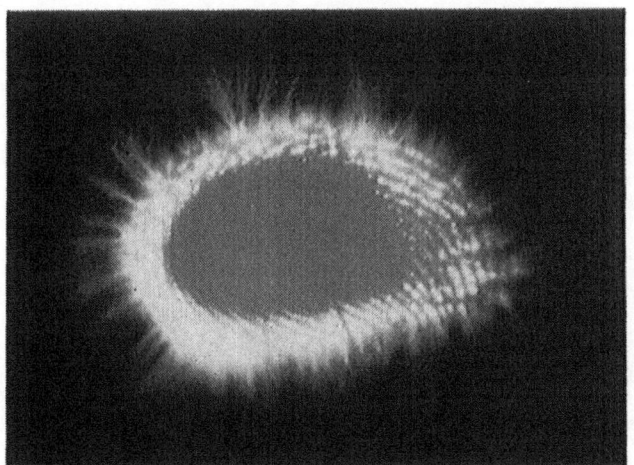

Forefinger of patient with Hodgkin's desease before radiation therapy.

Figure 1

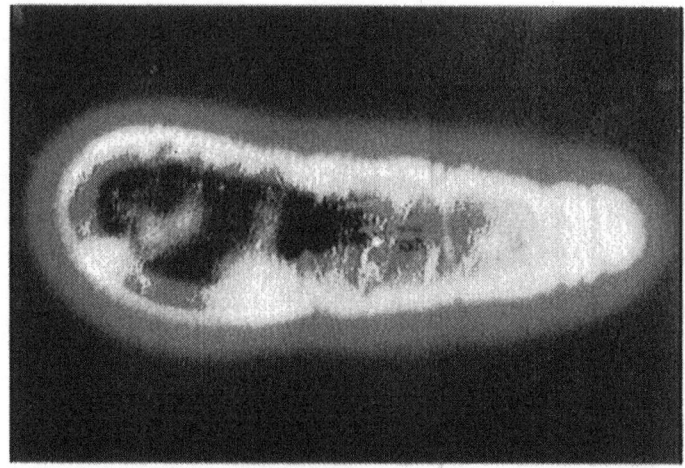

Forefinger of same patient after radiation therapy (Red corona due to reversed polarity of High Voltage power supply: usually blue)

Figure 2

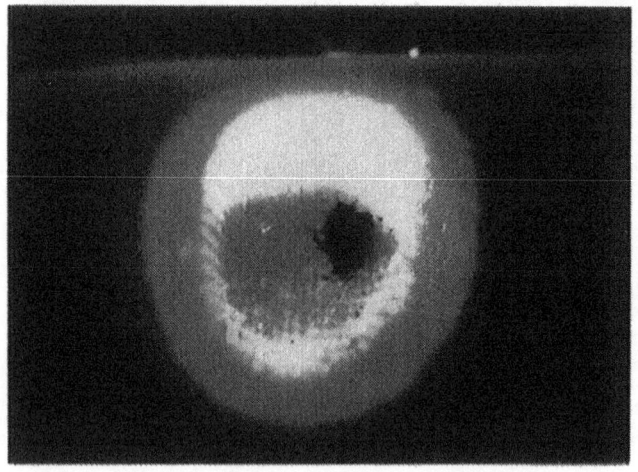

Forefinger of healer at rest (polarity reversed)

Figure 3

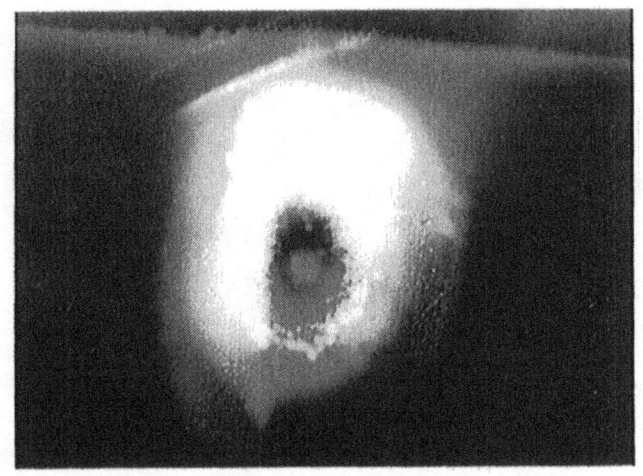

Forefinger of same healer thinking of healing
Figure 4

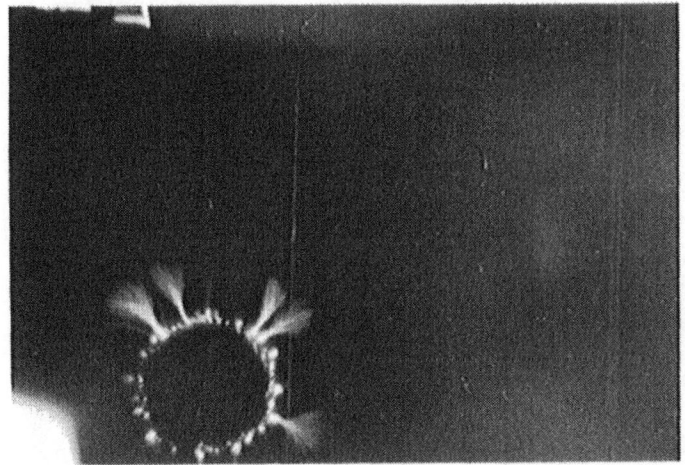

Forefinger of subject before hypnosis
Figure 5

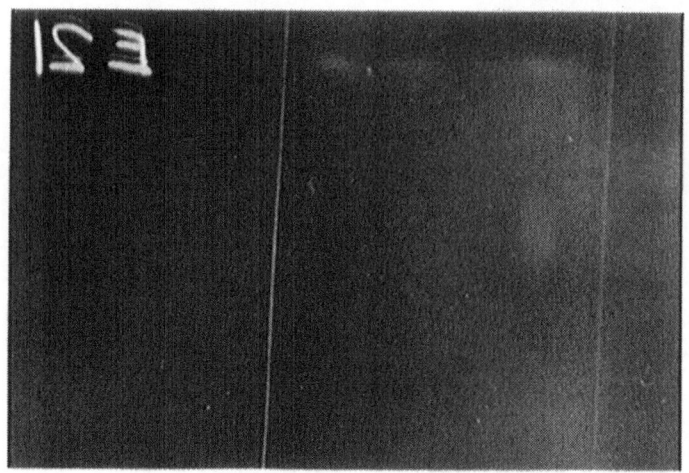

Same subject deep into hypnosis

Figure 6

Same subject in post-hypnotic state

Figure 7

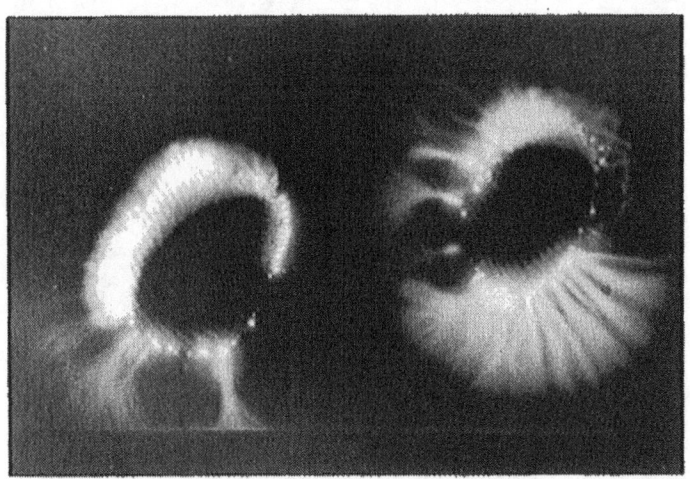

Forefinger of meditator concentrating on crown (top of the
Head) chakra

Figure 8

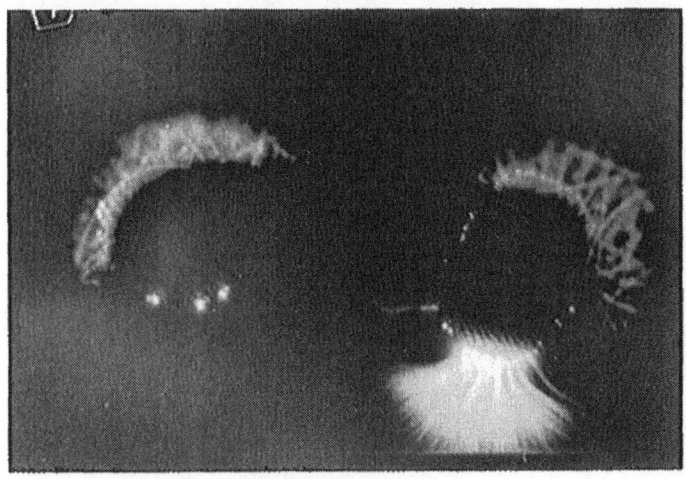

Same subject concentrating on base chakra

Figure 9

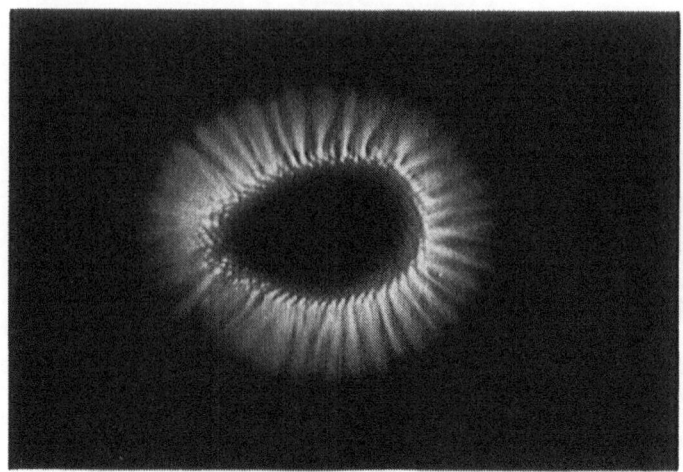

Forefinger of a meditator highly developed as a psychic who is concentrating on the crown chakra

Figure 10

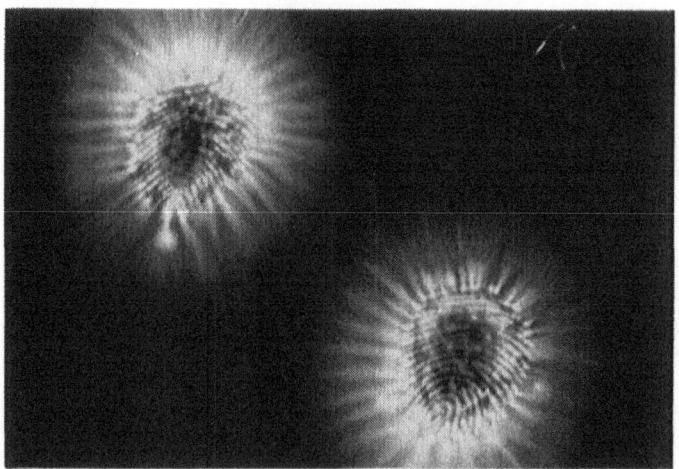

Same psychic meditator concentrating on base of spine chakra. Note similarity in this subject between crown and base chakras.

Figure 11

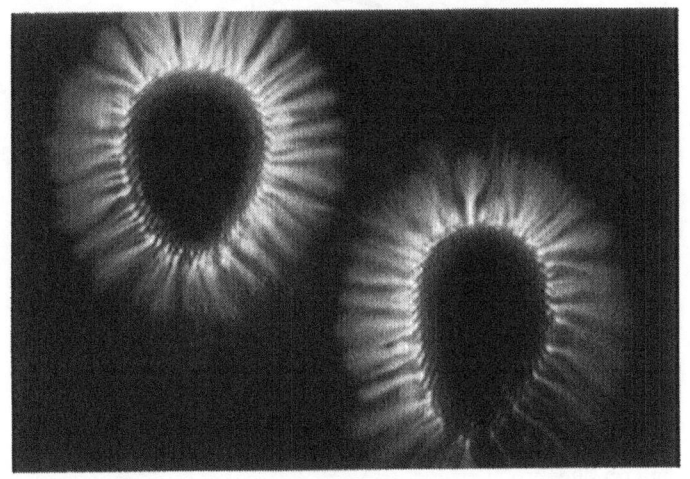

Base of spine chakra
Figure 12

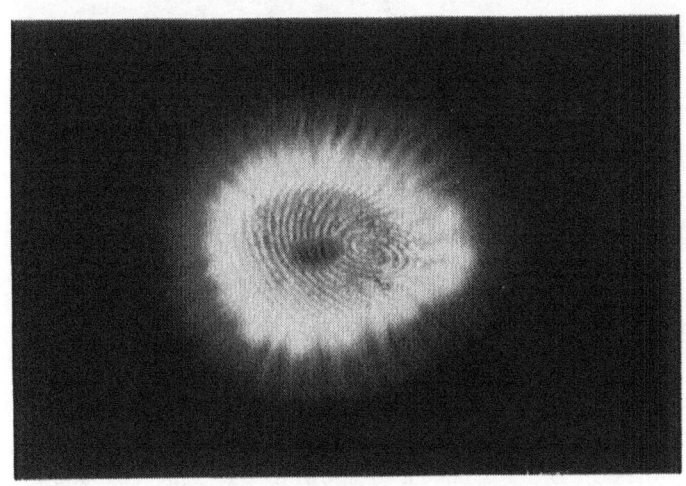

An evolved meditator deep in meditation.
Figure 13

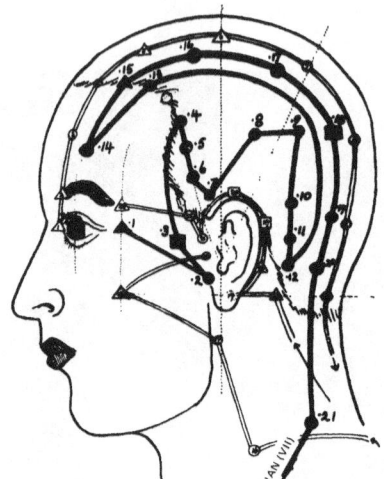

Diagram of certain acupuncture points including one centered high on cheek.

Figure 14

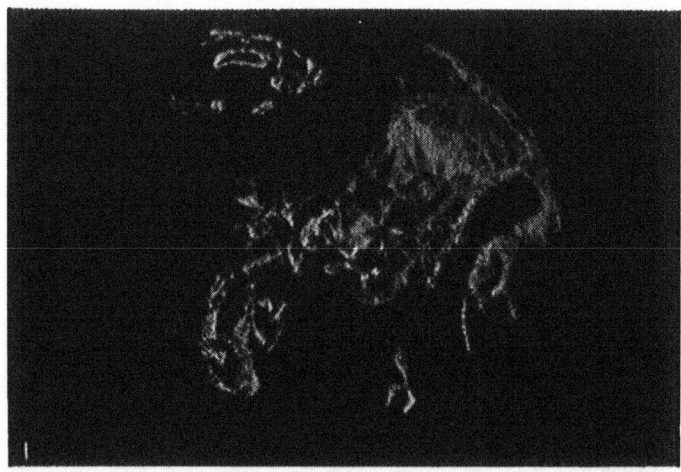

Lamar University Kirlian photograph of the profile of physics professor Dr. Joseph Pizzo showing the same acupuncture point as circled in Figure 14. From an 8" x 10" Ektachrome transparency wrapped around the face during a one minute exposure of 25,000 volts with a frequency of 7.7 Kilohertz.

Figure 15

think in terms of energy re-bounding between these "fields," we can better understand the need for balancing them. Since thoughts and emotions give off energy waves, they hereby are related to colors; the negative emotions such as anger and fear, show turbulent, dark patterns. These forms of negativity in time affect the health of the body as well as the mind—perhaps the darker colors actually hold off the finer light waves necessary even for energy, but this is metaphysical conjecture. Sensitives investigated by Dr. Shafica Karagulla did describe the finer sheaths penetrating and containing the grosser ones. The idea of man having bodies of increasingly finer substances, Ralph Metzner explains, is found in "esoteric Christianity, in occult philosophy and theosophy, in Gurdjieff, and in Actualism, (a yoga discipline taught by Russell Paul Schofield) where it is explained on the basis of different frequency rates." (*Maps of Consciousness*, 1971).

"He who knows the truth of the body can then come to know the truth of the universe," says the ancient Ratnasara Tantra. "The human body is a very special kind of transducer of the non-material aspect of the One energy into material manifestation," writes Dr. Herbert Puryear and Mark Thurston, interpreters of the Cayce material. Definite physical conditions take place within the inner man as an individual goes progressively into deep meditation. These conditions have been thoroughly investigated and explained by such teachers as Gopi Krishna and Roy Eugene Davis. It will help to understand the transforming energy called kundalini with which they deal, if we begin with the seven glands of the endocrine system.

In the Cayce readings these glands are described as contacts which, when properly attuned, bring in a flow of spiritual energy from God, the source of the One energy. In the Eastern tradition these seven glandular centers of energy are called "chakras" and correspond to the vortices of energy in the invisible "bodies" just discussed. The concepts of energy centers in the organism has yet to be accepted by physiologists; however, Ralph Metzner reports that individual scientists such as Robert O. Becker and

associates at the State University of New York Medical
Center, have, in their studies which deal with the direct
current potentials in amphibians and man, observed that
"a complex electrical field was found. . . and its spatial
configuration was noted to bear a close relationship to the
gross anatomic arrangement of the central nervous system." Metzner also relates that Wilhelm Reich found that
growth processes radiated outward from the center to the
periphery, with the flow of energy proceeding through a
number of what Reich called different "segments. . . ocular,
oral, thoracic, lumbar, sacral," and could be dammed up
or blocked at one or more of these segments. The reader
may also refer back to H.S. Burr's "fields of life" in
Chapter One.

The centers of energy which are believed to relate to the
endocrine glands are said in ancient tradition to have corresponding colors. Moving from the Gonads, to the Cells
of Leydig, to Adrenals, Thymus, Parathyroid and thyroid,
to the Pineal and Pituitary the colors were believed to range
from the lower frequency reds up to the lavenders and
violets. Studies which we recently conducted at the Lamar
University Physics Lab with physics professor Dr. Joseph
Pizzo seemed to bear out this color shift recorded by tradition and seen by sensitives. In color physics as we move
up the spectrum from infra red to violet and then to far
ultra-violet there is about a four-fold increase in energy,
from approximately one to about four electron volts. Similarly the colors seen by clairvoyants and recorded by Kirlian photography seem to show an energy increase from
the lower chakras to the higher. This energy was sampled
by finger-tip photos as the subject concentrated on the
various chakras. Moreover, some evidence supporting the
teaching of some esoteric groups, like the Summit Light-
house, was also noted: that in the advanced meditator or
person who had "purified" his use of energy, the color
around the crown and base of the spine would both be
white. Tradition says that when these two centers are properly balanced, the person will be able to transmit great
healing power. One can raise within himself, the Cayce

readings also state, "that which may be sent out as a power," and this force directed to one in need has tremendous healing energy.

Roy Eugene Davis, in describing the subtle nature of the chakras, feels they relate to the physical body at the various nerve ganglia, where they interact with some of the glands of the body. The energies that flow to the body through the chakras actually extend beyond the body as at the top of the head. This, when it is strong enough in intensity, has been recorded as the "halo" in paintings and sculptors of Christian, Indian and Tibetan saints. The crown chakra, Davis feels, is an ancient energy channel which opened to an external source. (*Darshan the Vision Of Light*, 1971).

You can think of the seven spiritual centers as knots up which you climb as each center is opened, says E.M. Baker, (*Edgar Cayce On Meditation*, 1974). While breathing exercises, chants, and incense help unlock the sleeping energy of "kundalini," caution is necessary. More gentle ways implicit in meditating on agape love—the unselfish compassionate love—will safely awaken and begin to attune the system. The energy of kundalini is a powerful one, and if awakened before a person has begun to be balanced, as is often the case with drug usage, the system can spin out of balance, so to speak. Kundalini expert Gopi Krishna believes that all manner of aberrations, perversions, and insanity can be attributed to the premature "opening" of the chakras, before ego, emotions, desires, and physical health are beginning to be brought under control of the higher Self.

The use of drugs to open the chakras is one of the high-risk approaches. The most forthright statement on drugs in relation to higher states of consciousness comes from Gopi Krishna:

These practices [drug taking] have been in vogue in India for many centuries without producing a single enlightened spirit. Drug-taking hermits number hundreds of thousands and are a source of unhappiness to themselves and to others.

Narcotics, hallucinogens, and intoxicants are not a help but
an insuperable barrier in the path of God-realization
("The True Aim of Yoga").

By now the reader has probably realized that we ourselves
consider the use of drugs the least valid route to expanded
consciousness. As we see it, the evidence does suggest that
many have known a temporary expansion of consciousness
by this means. On the other hand, continued use of drugs
to sustain the state results in negative results for personality.
In the last chapter it will be seen that authentic peak experiences have positive consequences for personality. The
worst problems of one young man we counselled stemmed
directly from his temporary "cosmic vision" through LSD
which all but overwhelmed his ego. During a difficult
period of two and a half years, we saw his personality
gradually recover its identity and discipline itself to the
extent that he could once again exercise his will to positive
ends on his daily life. But in the process he encountered
many months of his own private hell. The externals of his
life now suggest a fully functional personality; therefore, his
future spiritual growth now has a realistic foundation.

From our counselling experience, many young people
appear to have gotten the idea from such writers as Aldous
Huxley, Dr. John Lilly, and Carlos Castenada that drugs
are as valid as any other means to higher consciousness.
In this view, years of personal growth and discipline can
be dispensed with—a magic chemical will do the job. But as
Baba Ram Dass says in *Be Here Now*, "The goal is to
be high, not get high." Whatever his earlier experiences,
the path he finally found was the traditional, disciplined
one.

At the level of personality growth, the person whose sensitivity and sense of completeness is furnished by drugs or
alcohol has unfinished psychological work. Not only is the
entire energy system thrown off balance by the premature
opening of the chakras, but, drugs, being illegal, contribute
to paranoia. Young people have described paranoia-like
feelings even with marijuana. The longer but safer route

begins with balancing the chakras, then raising kundalini.

When kundalini begins to rise one will feel an almost electrical surge running along the spine. Many recommend teachers or gurus to help one deal with the increase of activity, energy, and abilities that the meditator will experience. Not only the fears and blocks we have built into these centers are unlocked as the energy rises, but the power and talents as well. A purification and transformation of man's "bodies" as well as the refinement of the nervous system takes place. Roy Eugene Davis writes, "As Kundalini moves through the vehicles of man, it purifies the passageways through which life-force flows and transforms man's bodies completely." In more scientific terms, the force fields of varying wave-lengths of energy around the body, which have been colored by emotions and desires are being changed. If the energy is allowed to come in through the heart chakra, by way of love, it can flow evenly to the lower centers related to sex, power, etc., and the upper centers of increased intution, insight, awareness and a cosmic consciousness. These higher centers will be robbed of energy if a man concentrates on the lower.

At each level of consciousness, you go through a major re-orientation. The ego experiences great instability, then gradually settles into the new level, provided that the growth is real. Ideally the growth problems of each level of consciousness should be completed before going ahead. Each level is keyed to its own chakra.

"The major portion of *Kundalini: Consciousness-energy at rest*," writes Roy Eugene Davis, "in the body of the average man is inactive. Such a one is still functioning primarily in the lower levels of consciousness." At these levels attention flows outward into involvement with externals. The greater portion remains inactive in the lower centers. This statement may lead the reader to wonder about the revolutionary sexual attitudes of the young and the claim of such methods as tantric yoga to achieve the higher states of consciousness. There seems to be a growing use of the random sexual experience among the young spiritual seekers of the population. The trend seems to go

hand in hand with the re-emphasis of the body as the vehicle by which inner growth takes place. Granted that the
body is important in the growth of consciousness, it does
not follow that it should be allowed to be the master of
reason and spiritual discipline. One must be, says the ancient *Bhagavad-Gita*, "a master of the senses" if one is
to realize the highest union of Self to all Being. Every culture throughout the world has restricting patterns of behavior; if nothing else, they serve as an indication of selfishness. How much is a man willing to restrict his behavior
in the interests of the feelings and expectations of others, and
to maintain order in society? We need to remember that
our ways in the West and our evolution of consciousness is
different; this does not prevent us from using enriching ideas
from other sources, but we should not apply them blindly.
Ralph Metzner feels that we can take the valuable essence
from the tantras and other ancient ways, test it, verify it
and convert it to our needs, all the while remembering an
old Indian proverb: "One must learn to protect himself
against the tigers to which one has given birth, as well as
against those begotten by others." We must discriminate in
accepting what is ours and what is not and eliminate the
"consuming" that "obstructs our growth."

In this connection it is well to remember again that energy will be where the interest is. Certainly one cannot
achieve the total illumination of the kundalini energy rising
to the Crown chakra while focusing it primarily at the
sexual level. Roy Eugene Davis quotes Yoganandaji's
comment to a young disciple who implied that the natural
drives were missing since his Master was a monk. "The
only difference between you and me," he replied, referring
to the sexual energy, "is that I meditate and draw the
energy up into the higher centers and then use it for creative work." Put in other terms, desires which are selfish
tend to limit the flow of information through the Unconscious—the level fully tuned to God.

In psychointegration an individual primarily at the
sexual and power levels typically exhibits maximum ego
inflation. In addition, even the ethic of such a stage of

consciousness seems to dominate him. At the sexual level, the ethic translates into "my sexual happiness is paramount, whatever the consequences for others." At the power level, the ethic is "the exercise of power over others is my right—I am the sole arbiter of its use." Of course, these assumptions are not on the conscious level, but are underlying assumptions when the psyche's energies are concentrated at these levels.

For many people who leave home to find their identities in the peer group, sexual experiences often seem to retard the unfolding of personality. When the only sharing is sexual, other facets of personality tend to be neglected. In the long run, the personality growth upon which spiritual experience must be based may be delayed. We have already given an illustration of this in our discussion of dream cases.

Some of the sanest comments on the whole subject of the male-female relationship are given in Roy Eugene Davis' book, *Darshan: The Vision Of Light.* In the hope of shedding light on the importance of true mating, we give them in full:

> When two people are properly mated, the result is true union and a powerful radiation flows through them. Psychic currents pass from one to the other on the physical, astral, and mental levels. This results, not in mere physical release, but in complete blending . . . . The male-female relationship is of vital importance even if the physical closeness is absent because there is an electrical interchange which takes place when understanding people share their love. A physical relationship is not always possible, or desired. Mere proximity is sufficient to allow positive and negative energies to comingle; this results in balance and fulfillment. Such a relationship softens a man's nature and give confidence and support to the woman . . . . Every man of accomplishment has had the right woman in his life to reinforce his nature and balance his energies. A man is not complete without his feminine counterpart and the reverse is also true.

The nearer one draws to the consciousness of the Divine,

the more power comes back through his life and circumstances. In this way body, mind and soul are spiritual-
ized or brought into perfect attunement with Spirit. One
becomes serene and relaxed, creativity is furthered and
mental processes become sharpened. "A man who becomes
serene, achieves inner order," says the sage Lao-Tse, "and
in this way his life—and everything in it—is in order. Those
who attain inner order produce effects upon their surroundings without acting by regenerating them through their
own beingness." (K.O. Schmidt, *Lao-Tse's Book of Life*,
1975.) If this sounds like mystical vagueness, one has only
to remember the glowing, regular finger-tip photographs
of the balanced person. The energy radiating from such a
person can heal another as dramatically as many of the
Biblical healings because such a one is energized by Spirit.
The impact of a well-ordered person will extend outward
from the family and friends to the state. Not only would a
world of well-organized persons bring peace, but it would
also affect the natural environment; as plant studies are
beginning to show that crops can be affected by man's
thinking. "Thoughts and images are formed into physical
reality and become fact," says Seth, (Jane Roberts, *Seth
Speaks*, 1972). "The only objective world is the end result of inner actions. . . . Your scientists will have to face
the fact that consciousness comes first and evolves its own
form."

Directions for finding the path of inner order are varied.
Desireless is the way, says the Tao. "Not considering anything outside as desirable thus one prevents anxiety and dis-
cord inside . . . . Unconcerned about gains and losses,
we experience fullness. By emptying ourselves, we become
magnetic for abundance . . . . A man who has recognized
the dynamics of serenity and emptiness . . . who is aiming
first of all at the Tao (the way) and is ordering his inner
life, orders and masters his outer life effortlessly and lives
in abundance." The principle here—which is the same as the
psychology found in "the Sermon On the Mount," i.e.,
"But seek ye first the kingdom of God and his righteous-

ness and all these things shall be added unto you.'' (Matthew 6:33)—is underscored by modern psychology, particularly in the thought of Carl Jung. The principle is letting go of one's ego, and though this ''letting-go'' is difficult for the West, it is the essence of non-attachment and letting-God-act. ''One must be able to let things happen in the psyche.'' (Carl Jung, ''Commentary on 'The Secret of the Golden Flower','' *Complete Works* XIII). The will may be applied actively in one's growth; yet, at some point, the will must stand aside.

Even biologically this truth is becoming demonstrable. Meditators, daily giving up will and its accompanying anxiety, gradually achieve greater physical health and mental ability. Emptied of ego, and with the growing strengthening of the nervous system, such a person begins to be a reflector of a higher energy and purpose.

> He who strives for the highest, will partake of the highest forces, and thereby he himself will move his limits into the infinite: he will realize the infinite in the finite, making the finite the vessel of infinity, the temporal the vehicle of the timeless.
>
> (Govinda, ''Light of Asia'' 1969)

Lama Govinda's statement is more than beautiful poetry. We are thinking in terms of being a vessel for a proven force, a force which is great enough to bring about healing and other so-called ''wonders.'' This force and its accompanying human counter-part, the awakened energy which the Eastern world calls kundalini, is just beginning to interest the scientific world.

Perhaps the best known writer on the subject of kundalini, Gopi Krishna, is adamant on the point that the awakened kundalini energy is the biological basis for all genius and creativity (*The Biological Basis of Religion and Genius*, 1971). He has worked in Switzerland with the distinguished German astrophysicist, Dr. Carl Friedrich Freiherr von Weizacker, and has founded ''The Research Institute of Kundalini'' in New York City, as well as centers in Europe and Canada. "The same biological center of energy in the body is responsible for both mystical experience and genius," he says, berating science for its past lack of serious investigation into the human mind, the mystical experience, and enlightened consciousness. More potent forms of biochemical substances are produced in the process of evolution, he feels, substances which act as fuel for psychic energy. Reminding us that our bodies are the most elaborate chemical laboratories on earth, so sensitive that a 300,000 part of a gram of LSD can alter human consciousness (in some cases leading to insanity, murder, or suicide), he urges serious investigation of the kundalini energy.

Manifestations of this energy have been documented in hundreds of authentic texts from prehistoric times in India, Tibet, China, Japan, and the middle East, and would have already created "a revolution in modern thought" except for being written in a cryptic form, Sandhya Bhasha. As he says, "Adept after adept in unambiguous terms has testified in recorded confessions to the existence and efficacy of this marvellous Psychosomatic Power Mechanism with awe and adoration and has treated it as an All-Intelligent and Omnipotent Divine Energy, the architect of every form of life in the universe. What is of particular interest, with special relevance to the problems of this age, is the fact that in hundreds of these writings the biological reactions, caused in the body on the arousal of the Power Center, have been described in unmistakable terms, the best that the general level of knowledge of these days allowed authors to do." Immersed in the subject since his first personal experience with it in 1937, Gopi Krishna's testimony is authoritative in this field.

Evidently, then, profound changes take place in the nervous system and brain of meditators over a period of time. The nervous system represents increasing complexity from the spinal cord upward through the brain stem and into the brain itself. The highest levels of the system, the brain itself, seems to be divided, at least in some functions, between the left and right hemispheres. We call the collection of these functions mind; what then is consciousness? In Anthony Campbell's opinion, the evidence seems to say that "Consciousness is not identical with the brain or mind but it is that which witnesses the changes which occur in brain and mind." Campbell sees the structure as a continuum: body (nervous system including the brain); the mind-consciousness. The sharpest division in the continuum is between mind and consciousness. The basis for this conception comes from the work of the surgeon, Dr. Wilder Penfield, who found that, with the direct stimulation of the brain in patients who were conscious during operations, there was the sensation of reliving past experiences though they were still aware of their present surroundings. "Something is understanding two conscious streams simultaneously and judging their relations to each other," says J.C. Eccles discussing this phenomenon; "We are still not either naming or identifying or understanding it" (*Brain and Conscious Experience*, 66).

Parapsychological research is showing that consciousness can operate externally from the body. This is the out-of-body experience. Could consciousness be, as the religions of the world have always maintained, an individual part of Universal Mind, Being, Love—whatever term one chooses? Maharishi says that individual consciousness is produced "by the reflection of the Absolute in a given nervous system," waiting, so to speak, for a properly tuned nervous system in order to be able to manifest. Those who could most perfectly reflect back the pure state of Universal Mind, would literally be filled with more energy, light, *Life!* The halos of white light around the heads of saints are saying something and understanding it would bring a new step in man's evolutionary journey.

"When kundalini is aroused and, over a period of time ascends to the crown chakra," writes Roy Eugene Davis, "the mystic marriage is consummated." The ecstasy, fulfillment and awe which this experience brings, as anyone who is familiar with it will know, surpasses all other sense experiences. It transcends anything known on earth, Gopi Krishna agrees, creating feelings of "overwhelming love,

dependence and utter surrender." He cites the recorded experiences of the Christian mystics such as St. Paul, St.
Francis of Assisi, St. Teresa, Dionysius the Areopagite,
St. Catherine of Siena, Suso and others, and Sufi Masters
including Shamsi-Tabrez, Rumi, Abu Yazid, al-Nure, and
al-Junaid, and also the experiences of yoga adepts such as
Kabir, Guru Nanak, Shankaracharya, Ramakrishna,
Maharishi Ramana and others to show that, in the essen-
tials, the basic experience is the same. With the rising of
the kundalini to the crown chakra there is the building of
the "wedding garment" which we read of in the New Tes-
tament, without which no man goes to the wedding feast.

"In this last state of love," says St. John of the Cross,
"the soul is like the crystal that is clear and pure; the more
degrees of light it receives, the greater concentration of
light there is in it. This enlightenment continues to such a
degree that at last it attains a point at which the light is
centered in it with such copiousness that it comes to appear
to be wholly light and cannot be distinguished from the
light . . . ." Both Christ and the Buddha spoke of being the
light. "No follower of mine shall wander in the dark; he
shall have the light of life," Jesus said.

For good reason, then, light has been an almost universal symbol among Christians, Jews, Zorastrians, Buddhists, and many others. It symbolizes deep certainties which
lie below consciousness. This universally-described illumination transcends ideologies, religious dogmas, and all other
divisive influences which separate mankind. Only under its
influence can mankind achieve unity on the planet. In *The
Infinite Way* we find these ideas expressed very beautifully.
This illuminated state "has no ritual or rule but divine,
impersonal Love; no other worship than the inner Flame
that is ever lit at the shrine of spirit. This union is the free
state of spiritual brotherhood. The only restraint is the discipline of Soul, therefore we know liberty without license;
we are a united universe without physical limits; a divine
service to God without ceremony or creed. The illuminated
walk without fear—by Grace."

The spiritual adept or religious genius is rare, says Gopi Krishna, because his illumination represents a transformation of consciousness, "the opening of a new channel of perception within by which the deathless and boundless universe is opened to the vision of the soul . . . . The average man, oblivious to his own divine nature and unconscious of his own majesty, lives in permanent doubt because of the limitations of the human brain. He is overwhelmed by uncertainty and sorrow at the though of death and identifies with the body from first to the last." For this reason all religious disciplines and systems of yoga are designed to bring about the changes in the body, psychomatic changes, which "are essential for the metamorphosis of consciousness" and the activation of a new center presently dormant in the average man and woman. Activating this dormant center so that "a more powerful stream of psychic energy (can) rise into the head from the base of the spine (will) enable human consciousness to transcend the normal limits. This is the final phase of the present evolutionary impulse in man." ("The True Aim Of Yoga," *Psychic Magazine,* Jan-Feb., 1973) For further enlightenment on the radical change which man's cerebral-spinal system must undergo to allow consciousness to reach a dimension beyond the highest intellect, the reader may refer to "Kundalini: Key To Evolution," by Gopi Krishna (*Psychic,* April, 1972).

As we said earlier, a strong enough surge of agape love will pull the energy upwards. Loving one another is the most important and fruitful activity that any on earth can offer. By love we are created and molded. By love we are carried forward from this world to the next. Love suffers much in order to provide the necessary elements for existence.

In the act of meditating let your thoughts run over the whole range of what has been provided for you on this earth through love. Some of you who have lived long enough or thought deeply enough will begin to see the working of love throughout the tempestuous and stormy scenes you have encountered along the way. In love there is always a chance for growth. Without love our fates would be settled and hard, if we had existence at all. Love helps us conquer our faults by supplying us with forebearance and patience. Love never omits tests that are necessary for the development of the individual.

We speak of love in these terms as a force behind the universe that is so constructed as to be aware of the needs of each member participating in life. By love you are molded, by love you are raised up. By love you are succored from the beginning.

Let your hearts be guided by love for under its influence you can achieve monumental tasks. Do you want fame, fortune, and wealth? Then seek to use these for the benefit of others. Likewise endure with patience the torments of watching others grow. There is no growth that does not involve risk. In the endeavors of others see the same potential as you would develop within yourself. All works for the fulfillment of man's understanding and no judgment should be applied to the path another chooses for learning. Love is the inheritance of the universe.

The reader may be interested in knowing that the above passages as well as the pages which follow were received during creative meditation.

To love is to know God. To last in the face of adversity is to proclaim the strength of spirit of which you and all mankind are a part. Nothing and no one can come between those hearts and minds attuned to God-love and God-service. For the very power that draws these upward, proves to be its own progenitor. If you will wait for the stir of Spirit within your life, and it will come as body and mind are tuned to the harmony implicit in each individual. Your way will be made clear. Spirit equals Life equals Illumination; an increased flow of spirit means increased life, motivation, joy and energy. Meditation has existed throughout the centuries of man's experience upon the earth, as a signpost which marks the spiritual path. Love is the way as well as the goal of this path. It will guide your steps into the true fulfillment and freedom.

These words are but encouragements until the time when they become reality, as they will for all seeking truth. Then, as the doors are opened into the illumined light of consciousness, you will well understand the magnificent mystery which you are.

On earth, life offers many alternatives. One can choose justice, forebearance, the way of right action, or succumb to the negative traits—selfishness, obesity, anger, inner turmoil. Each man finds himself confronted with inharmonious situations, but it is only by working through these that he can realize his true stature. Those who fail choose not to try hard enough. The way of failure is, in itself, a lesson.

Learning to proceed cautiously in life is necessary and will eliminate many of the irrational impulses from one's consciousness. As one progresses, he will deliver himself more willingly to be a channel of usefulness to others.

Remember, the goal is union with the universal consciousness, and it is, as Gopi Krishna says, a herculean achievement more full of adventure and thrill than the longest voyage in outer space, "the greatest enterprise designed by nature for the most virile and most intelligent members of the race . . . ."

"Thou art that," says Hindu wisdom. "All men are inherently divine, but they come into their inheritance when they recognize it, identify themselves with it, and carry out the divine will." It is this identity that meditation helps you achieve. "Meditation is to make the individual conscious of his universal origin." (Govinda).

Above all meditation is a discipline. To still the clatter of the ego's consciousness, to listen, to look in the hope of hearing and seeing that which is more true than what the individual ego knows, all this requires discipline.

We live in an age which reveres freedom. The meaning of freedom for many is but the right sought by the ego to do as it pleases. But this is slavery for the higher Self. In this situation it is difficult to explain a higher freedom known for centuries. It is the freedom to seek to know the harmony of the universe and to choose to align oneself with that harmony. In earlier times this was described as seeking to know the will of God and then choosing to accept that will.

Undeniably, discipline is the first step in any spiritual quest, in any intellectual quest or any artistic one. Any process that enables one to begin the discipline of body, mind, and emotions should be begun at once, for it will begin to break the chains that false thinking and acting have set in motion. Each day set some goal of achievement, no matter how minor it is. Look back at the end of the day to see what got in the way, if it was not achieved. Learn to see the ways in which emotions pulled you in self-defeating directions, and discriminate in the use of those emotions which left you feeling strengthened and fortified.

The great need for mankind in this hour on earth is not to sink into a morass of negative emotions, no matter how much circumstances seem to warrant them. You have the key to your own victory within yourself, a mystery which will unfold as you put into practice the thinking and doing that has been suggested. You will be joining, as you try, a host of valiant souls whose lives have crossed this earth— who have left a bit of themselves and their wisdom behind as a light for others. You are not alone and you can reach for perfection.

Chapter V
Ultraconsciousness

The conception of personality upon which this book is based, that is, psychointegration, is in essence a rhythm, an evolutionary rhythm. First, there is an expansion into the life of the senses, the material world, the biological and cultural goals; second, there is a contraction which ultimately can take one into the temple. In the second stage, priorities reverse. The goal becomes the spiritual quest for the One. By now we have made it sufficiently clear that the temple is within. Literally—you are the mystery.

In personality terms the first movement is toward individuality and this means the working out of the fully functioning ego. Then in the return, there is a developing awareness of the mystery within, the Self, in relation to which the ego is but the manager, the Self, the owner. Realization of this fact is indispensable for entry into the temple—and attunement to the One. In psychointegration, the moment of attunement is an experience at the seventh level of consciousness. While the individual afterward returns to a lower level, he has been transformed and his life enriched. Many do not complete the rhythm, but enough have done so that its ultimate worth is clear. The foregoing chapters have shown an increasing awareness of the temple by many on the frontiers of science. The reader has also been given many insights into the various successful techniques by which he can prepare himself for his own entrance into the temple. He also has probably become aware of the necessity for discipline, patience, and a healthy outlook toward the suffering which all inevitably experience.

Within the temple, though the experience varies greatly, the most useful and, we believe, the most descriptive term is "ultraconsciousness." It was coined by the Miami, Florida psychiatrist, Dr. Stanley R. Dean. In this state, for a brief time, the limits of ordinary consciousness drop away, the limitations of personality are transcended, and the individual is privileged for a moment of clarity, to lock into the harmony of the universe. Later, when trying to analyze that which is beyond human analysis, he will at the least recover his perception of the limitless love and the hugely conceived moral order of the universe. If he recounts visual imagery, light and color beyond previous conception are typical.

Often the experience of ultraconsciousness will include the temporary removal of consciousness from the physical body—or what is called the out-of-body experience. It is as if the moment is too powerful for the body or its ego. The ego's limited and personal conception of reality seems endangered by this instant of cosmic consciousness. Despite the literally awesome nature of ultraconsciousness, it is the natural culmination of personal growth and has enriched the lives of millions. It should be emphasized that such enlightenment has been much more widely experienced than previously recognized. In 1974 the University of Chicago's National Opinion Research Center conducted an in-depth national survey of 1500 Americans. The sociologist, Reverend Andrew Greely, who supervised the survey said, "Thirty-six per cent of Americans interviewed say they have, at some time in their lives, felt as though they were close to a powerful force that seemed to lift them out of themselves." Significantly none of the subjects connected drug usage to this peak experience.

The obvious reason that society is ignorant of the depth and extent of ultraconsciousness is that its cultural assumptions cause it either to deny the reality of the experience or to ascribe the peak experience to mental illness. The Scottish psychiatrist, Dr. R. D. Laing, writing in the preface to

The Divided Self (1965), took his departure from Freud's view of the repressive nature of civilization where instincts are concerned, then said: ''Our civilization represses not only the 'instincts,' not only sexuality, but any form of transcendence. Among one-dimensional men, it is not surprising that someone with an insistent experience of other dimensions, that he cannot entirely deny or forget, will run the risk either of being destroyed by the others, or of betraying what he knows.''

At least where mystical experience is concerned, this hostility on the part of society appears to be changing. Faced with the existential crisis of meaning of the latter part of this century, a crisis in which the conventional values of society are threadbare, the search for new meaning is leading to a new openness. We have tried to show the signs of this new development. In such a climate many are beginning to realize that personal survival and growth are dependent upon what they are able to do about their own inner unfolding.

How did we lose this essential knowledge? As we have observed repeatedly, the ancients possessed it. Furthermore awareness of the meaning of both inner growth and ultra-consciousness continued into relatively recent times. Finally, however, science in its eagerness to learn about the outer physical universe denied the reality of the inner universe. Thus the temple was eclipsed. Generations of ministers, themselves becoming ignorant of the temple because their awareness of its beauties was only second-hand, at length began teaching a religion stripped of all but ethical content. Ethical precepts lose their force when the larger basis of love is lost. This process has gone so far in this country that we now see the absurd situation in which a major department of the executive branch of the federal government has instituted workshops in honesty. Obviously institutional religion reduced to ethical precepts has lost any prospect of vital communication with the population. Ralph Waldo Emerson was aware that the lack of renewing experience within the church of his day had dehydrated it. Before the middle of the nineteenth century he wrote, ''an institution is the lengthened shadow of one man.'' At some point without continued personal experience within the inner temple, the institution succumbs to dry rot. Thus both the church as an institution and science, each for their own reasons, have tended to eclipse the reality of spiritual experience, particularly from the nineteenth-century on. But even the dry rot of an institution has its uses. An old stump can be the support of new growth using the stump's biological momentum for its own unfolding. So with institutions, and such is the case now. The spiritual impulse of the Unconscious is now seen to be a vital force pushing many into paths outside the whited sepulchre of the institutional church, paths which lead to the inner temple. Workers at the frontiers of science, particularly in theoretical physics, are beginning to sense what one of their pioneers, Albert Einstein, earlier called the ''irreducible mystery of the universe.'' This surely constitutes spiritual awareness.

A contemporary novel by the British writer, William Golding, *Free Fall* (1960), dramatizes the way in which authentic spiritual experience can come even to the most unlikely person under the right circumstances. This fictionalized version is a perfectly valid account of the process. It will be recalled that Saul, later Paul, was overwhelmed by ultraconsciousness on the road to Damascus. In his life, as is often the case, the transforming power of this state of consciousness radically reoriented his personality and goals. Embarked on a persecution of Christians, he became, instead, their leader. In Golding's novel, the hero is also very worldly. Sammy Mountjoy, the protagonist of *Free Fall,* by society's standards was a successful personality. Yet, despite his substantial ego satisfactions in the world, when subjected to physical isolation and darkness as a prisoner of war, he discovers that after all he is hollow within. He is a famous British artist; his paintings have been hung in the Tate in London. He has a very successful marriage, at least in sexual terms, yet finally his inner resources prove inadequate to withstand the psychological pressures of a German concentration camp. His interrogator, Dr. Halde, a former university psychologist, accurately gauges Sammy's essential hollowness, then deliberately induces a psychological crisis to break Sammy. Dr. Halde seeks certain information relating to camp security and has chosen Sammy as the weak link in the prison underground.

Sammy's ensuing crisis corresponds to the major crisis of individuation in psychointegration. There are many lesser crises. The major event typically occurs at the onset of the second half of life as the life rhythm begins its contraction phase. Depending upon the relative degree of maturity and the preparation for inner growth, the major crisis produces a variety of responses. These range from a neurosis (which may deepen into the night journey of the soul before its resolution produces growth) to a major identity crisis and suicidal despair. Of course, one may continue to sail on the surface of life, pursuing goals set from outside by one's peer group or the larger society. In this case there will often be an ever-deepening ennui, or world-weariness. While in its grip one has the nagging suspicion that life has much more to offer. The neurotic response to the fact of one's fortieth birthday is one symptom of the major individuation crisis. In many cultures the blind worship of the beauty of youth as opposed to the wisdom of age certainly intensifies this response.

In Golding's novel, the hero Sammy does not stop with self-pity. A traumatic childhood experience with darkness and loneliness heightens his terror at being alone in a dark cell—Dr. Halde's method of achieving psychological mastery of Sammy. The interrogator knew his man; Sammy is the poet T.S. Eliot's "Hollow Man" twenty years later in the deepening crisis of western values. Alone in the dark cell, his artist's imagination finishes Dr. Halde's work. Reduced to stark, insane terror, Sammy's instinct for survival functions: he cries for help. Help is forthcoming. His instinct thus leads him into the temple where he achieves transcendence.

Later, when he is released from what has proven to be only a broom closet, he returns to a different world. The experience of ultraconsciousness literally allows him to view a new reality. Circumstances and the state of his personality have combined to arrange a peak experience for him. As a consequence his personality is transcended. Pushing aside the curtains of his ego's selfishness, he looks out on a world which he has never seen. As he looks he perceives that for the rest of his life the main task is to get himself (his ego) "out of the way of that shining, singing cosmos and let it shine and sing." His new vision of the cosmos impels him to seek harmony with it. He recognizes that to do this means outgrowing his selfishness. From power over others he turns to the search for unselfish love (agape instead of eros love). He has come to see this type of love as the basis of a "vital morality, not the relationship of a man to remote posterity nor even to a social system, but the relationship of individual man to individual man." Because of ultraconsciousness, this new insight was forced to the center of his consciousness; the individual to individual relationship was observed to be "the forge in which all change, all value, all life is beaten out into a good or bad shape."

Before this breakthrough, Sammy had construed love in purely sexual terms and then, predictably, as self-satisfaction. Afterwards as a "burning amateur," he sought to love all others as he had earlier loved himself. This personality change cannot truly be affected from without. Laws, rules, authority, none of these can really make us love one another. Yet if we do not, our civilization may pass into oblivion. The end will have come from an ever-deepening selfishness. When the material goods of a just civilization become more important than kindness and consideration of others, society seems to regress to the jungle. The crucial value of ultraconsciousness for mankind should be evident.

For the individual within society, ultraconsciousness is no less vital. Sammy Mountjoy's functional response to the major crisis of individuation was fortunate, especially in view of the emptiness of his personality. Through his response to terror (the cry for help) he was enabled to transcend his egocentric life style, to behold with love the power and the glory of each individual's soul and thereby to assume responsibility for all of his own actions, even those in the past. These positive characteristics help distinguish the authentic from psychotic imitations of ultraconscious-ness. In another era Sammy might have founded a new church; instead he foreshadows the innumerable experiences of ultraconsciousness which will light man's way in the remaining years of this century. The author's vision expressed in his fictional character's growth marks a momentous historical transition. It is a turning from the authoritarian religious institutions of the Piscean Age to the individual, existential spiritual experience of the Aquarian Age. In *Free Fall* Golding foresees a bridge between science and religion. The individual who has known ultraconsciousness, because he has however briefly attuned with the cosmos, requires no such bridge. Experientially he has passed beyond the historical dilemma.

On top of the positive benefits already described, the person also experiences a release of latent creativity, intellectual power, and psychic gifts such as clairvoyance. Any or all of these may enrichen his personality. In addition he typically feels compelled to share the new vision; this desire is facilitated by his outer radiance, strength, and joy, all of which attracts others. These latter characteristics again help to distinguish the mystical state from pathological states.

All of these indicators are found throughout most cultures; thus ultraconsciousness is one of mankind's experiences which transcends dogma and geography. For the Christian it is known as the mystical experience, the Hindu calls it *Samadhi* (itself a matter of degree), and the Zen Buddhist labels it *satori*. Because of its universality, its cultivation will certainly work toward planetary harmony.

Although Eastern and Western descriptions of ultraconsciousness closely parallel one another, we have seen that the paths to the peak differ. The Christian speaks of coming into a ''state of grace'' which may descend upon him without preparation as it did for Paul on the road to Damascus. On the other hand, a follower of any of the Eastern religions typically disciplines himself in the expectation of enlightenment. He also thinks of various life practices which tradi-

tionally prepare him for the light. In the East, then, the
initiative lies more with the individual. For example, we
have spoken of the yogi who may follow any of a number
of physical, mental, and spiritual disciplines to this end. The
Christian is apt to be somewhat more passive as he awaits
the Holy Spirit. The contrast is, however, more apparent
than real. Some within the Christian church have also
utilized preparatory techniques. *The Spiritual Exercises of
St. Ignatius* (1962) is an example of published procedures.
In the West, however, really rigorous preparation probably
tends to be confined to those in holy orders.

The contrast between Plotinus, a follower of Plato who
attempted to reconcile Eastern teachings, Platonic thought
and Christianity, and Saint Augustine (354-430 A.D.),
the early Christian church father strongly influenced by
Plotinus, is illustrative of the Eastern and Western approaches. In addition to the influence on Christianity
through Augustine, Plotinus' thought as formalized in the
Neo-Platonism which was revived in the English Renais-
sance by the Cambridge Platonists continued on in the
work of nineteenth-century British romantic poets such as
Shelley. The influence of Plotinus upon the church itself
was to intensify its mystical side. Although Aristotle's rational, analytical approach later became ascendant within
the church in such thinkers as Saint Thomas Aquinas
(1225-1274), the mystical approach injected by Augustine
survives in contemporary mystics like Merton.

Central statements of Plotinus' mysticism are found in
The Enneads, particularly in a rather short essay, "The
Soul's Descent into Body." A synopsis of Greek attempts to
explain the "why" of the soul's descent into matter, into
flesh, is found here. Here also Plotinus establishes his
authority by describing his own mystical experiences:

> Many times it has happened, lifted out of the body into
> myself becoming external to all other things and self-en-
> centered. Beholding marvelous beauty; then more than ever,
> assured of community with the loftiest order [a momentary
> return to the One]. Enacting the noblest life. Acquiring

identity with the divine, stationing within It by having attained that activity. Posed above whatsoever within the Intellectual is less than the Supreme: yet there comes the moment of descent from intellection to reasoning, after that sojourn in the the divine, I ask myself how it happens that I can now be descending.

When Plotinus explores this topic in the writings of Greek thinkers and his own thoughts, a common theme emerges: the guilt of the soul acquired in the descent. This compares with the same concept in Pauline Christianity but Paul adds the idea that the descent of the soul fulfills the divine plan.

It will be recalled that language is inadequate to give a full account of the ultraconscious state. Thus it is not surprising that Plotinus often expresses his personal experiences in various metaphors. Three central metaphors have been identified by one of his commentators, Paul Henry, S.J. who wrote the introduction to the Faber and Faber edition of *The Enneads* (1962). The first metaphor is that of the rise and fall: ''the road is an ascent, a movement upward from below, increase of intensity and of concentration is a rise; dispersion and diminution of the mystical experience is a fall,'' a fall that is, from the peaks of ultraconsciousness. When Augustine later describes the same state of consciousness, he says ''thus invited to retreat into myself, I penetrated to the innermost part of my being, and I saw shining about my spirit, an unchangeable light.''

In the second metaphor ''external'' is contrasted with ''internal.'' According to Plotinus, the ascent is to be achieved through purification, the removal of external accreted to the internal or inmost self. The descent tarnishes the inner self. In the nineteenth century Ralph Waldo Emerson would later distinguish between the Me and the Not Me, the latter composed of the body, the personality and the external world. For Emerson the Me is the portion of the ''Over Soul'' within us, or as some would say, the Christ consciousness within. In psychointegration this is the Self. We have suggested that when the need for purification is misunderstood, the result can be a sterile asceticism which ignores the vital role of the body as the vehicle for consciousness. On the other hand, as we have also suggested, the reaction to asceticism can reduce one to a slavery of the senses and emotions. In either event, the growth of consciousness is retarded. The ascetic tendency of Pauline Christianity has probably contributed to the present confusion. Ultimately we cannot escape recognition of the essential truth of the Greek ideal: balance of body, mind, and spirit, understood in modern terms. Spiritual growth through meditation requires a healthy body and mind; on the other hand, purification through fasting and other disciplines is a necessary preparatory process. Obviously the requisite balance is a subtle problem which each must determine for himself.

The metaphysical implications of Plotinus' metaphors (ascent and purification) are "elevation," moving up to a peak experience, and "introversion," seeking the center. As Paul Henry points out, these metaphysical implications are compatible with Christian mysticism. A third metaphor, the return of the soul to its divine origins, is acceptable only in the sense that God is the creator of the human soul. We are now approaching what appears to be the essential distinction between Eastern and Western mysticism. It is to be seen in the following comparison of key statements by Plotinus and Augustine. First, Plotinus: "Now call up all your confidence; you need a guide no longer. See the soul, then, almost independent, almost on its own initiative." Then Augustine: "I entered even into my inward self, thou being by guide. And able I was for thou art become my helper." In the Eastern tradition as it comes into the thought of Plotinus, the individual seems less dependent on external assistance.

For traditional Christianity the most obvious external is the institutional, hierarchical church with much theology accreted to the text, itself versions of the actual spiritual experience. Consider, for instance, the various accounts of the life of Jesus in the four Gospels. An uneasy tension can develop for the individual who experiences ultraconsciousness. The tension arises betwen the external and the internal authority of direct, spiritual experience. A person suffused with direct, experiential knowledge presents some challenge at the least to the earthly authority of the church. As a consequence it seems that the church has never been at ease with these people. It may be completely unjust but one has the suspicion that the hierarchy is much happier with a dead saint than a live one. The monk, Thomas Merton, teaching Zen to nuns is one thing; Merton dead and revered for his life of devotion and spiritual writings is another. Whatever the avenue of expression, the live genius is always troublesome to the established social order in which he finds himself.

Despite the inevitable tension, the church in the West has often even included mystics among its leaders. This was the case even in seventeenth-century American Calvinism. The stereotype of the rigid Puritan into which history usually fits the great preacher, Jonathan Edwards (1703-1758), is, we find, not entirely useful. Edwards presents the contradiction of having been our most original American philosopher and having preached hell fire and damnation mons like "Sinners in the Hands of an Angry God." This is the sermon in which even the little children of his congregation are asked to visualize their souls as loathsome spiders dangling over the fiery pit.

By seventeen years of age Edwards, spurred by inner experience, had reasoned out probably the only viable basis for ethical conduct in his essay, "The Nature of True Virtue" (1765). The love of the cosmos, directly known by him, "benevolence to the sum of being," was the example. This love, expressed by the individual as agape love to all others would insure true virtue or "disinterested benevolence" to all. His later brimstone sermons perhaps grew out of his concern for souls, not the psychological comfort of his listeners. Unfortunately, his love led him to inculcate a religion of fear.

Edwards' best insights, on the other hand, such as his conception of the true moral basis of the universe, love, still possess validity. While his teachings were warped by the austere Puritan culture and theology, his highest ideas were the product of the intense Puritan religious practice which opened him to ultraconsciousness. In this way Edwards at his best was able to transcend the stultifying influence of Puritan theology in his philosophy.

Edwards records his encounters with ultraconsciousness in "A Personal Narrative." The ineffability of such events is evident in the language of his account:

> Not long after I began to experience these things, I gave an account unto my father of some things that passed into my mind. I was pretty much affected by the discourse we had together and when the discourse was ended, I walked abroad alone in a solitary place in my father's path to contemplation, and as I was walking there looking up on the sky and clouds, there came into my mind so sweet a sense of glorious *majesty* and *grace* of God that I know not how to express. I seemed to see them both in a sweet conjunction; majesty and deepness joined together; it was a sweet and gentle and holy majesty; a high great and holy gentleness.

The paradoxical nature of such a state, its ineffable quality, its exaltation transcending ordinary emotions, all these qualities strain language. Despite this difficulty, Edwards is sharing first-hand experience:

> Once, as I rode out into the woods for my health, in 1737, having alighted from my horse in a retired place, as my manner commonly has been, to walk for divine contemplation and prayer, I had a view that for me was extraordinary, of the glory of the son of God, as Mediator between God and man . . . . I felt an ardency of soul to be, what I know not otherwise how to express, emptied and annihilated . . . .

This particular event lasted for about an hour during which the emotional intensity was such that Edwards wept aloud.

Edwards was not alone in such states of consciousness. Edward Taylor (c. 1645-1729) who preceded Edwards, gives us an authentic experience of ultraconsciousness in the first stanza of his poem, "The Experience":

> Oh! that I always breath'd in such an aire,
> As I suckt in, feeding on sweet Content!
> Disht up unto my Soul ev'n in that pray're
> Pour'de out to God over last Sacrement.
> What Beam of Light wrapt up my Sight to finde
> Me neerer God than ere Came in my Minde?

The colonial period in America also included the Quaker movement, a religious group which put great stress upon the individual experience, the opening to the Inner Light. The effect of ultraconsciousness working through personality upon the larger society can be seen in the fact that one of the earliest critics of the institution of slavery in the New World was the Quaker tailor, John Woolman (1720-1772).

The diluting effect of the Age of Reason on American spiritual life accounts for a temporary decline of accounts of the mystical experience. This continued until the Transcendental movement launched by Ralph Waldo Emerson in the 1830's, when, once again, Eastern mysticism affected Western consciousness. Emerson drew great inspiration from the East, particularly the Hindu *Bhagavad-Gita*. Often accused of a facile optimism, especially in recent years, Emerson in fact had fought down many personal tragedies, much personal hardship, and great religious doubt to earn his cosmic perspective. His was a joy and optimism derived from his own inner experiences.

An important source of Emerson's perspective was the Hindu concept of the slow evolution of the soul through many lifetimes. In anticipation of later thinkers such as Carl Jung, Emerson began a meaningful distinction between the impermanent (the body, its personality), "the Not Me," and the permanent (the soul, part of the Over Soul), "the Me." Jung's later distinction was between the ego and the Self. Emerson's writings contain memorable expressions of ultraconsciousness such as: "Standing on the bare ground . . . all mean egotism vanishes. I become a transparent eyeball; I am nothing; I see all; the currents of the Universal Being circulate through me; I am part and parcel of God." (*Nature*, 1836)

Emerson inspired many of his younger contemporaries

to find and express their own portion of the Over Soul. Two of them were to make major literary contributions to the spiritual evolution of the West. Henry David Thoreau, as he wrote *Walden*, used the metaphor of fishing in Walden Pond to describe his own approach to cosmic consciousness. Walt Whitman's poem, "Song of Myself," seemingly an expression of personal egoism, is actually a hymn of praise to an emerging new nation and a joyous acceptance of the cosmic plan.

The reader will recall that ultraconsciousness leads the individual to a greatly expanded consciousness. He may not always be able to implement it in his life, but it nonetheless provides him direction. In the case of these writers it also produced great art. Theirs was an art which reveals the sense of what a friend of Whitman, the Canadian psychiatrist, Dr. R.M. Bucke, would later call "cosmic consciousness." Cosmic consciousness is to be seen in a few lines from Whitman's poem, "Passage to India."

> "Away O Soul! hoist instantly the anchor!
> Cut the hawsers—haul out—shake out every sail!
> Have we not stood here like trees in the ground long enough?
> Have we not grovel'd here long enough, eating and drinking
>   like mere brutes?
> Have we not darken'd and dazed ourselves with books
>   long enough?

The first edition of Dr. Bucke's book, *Cosmic Consciousness,* appeared in 1900. Ten years earlier he was president of the forerunner of the American Psychiatric Association. In 1894 he presented a paper on cosmic consciousness to this body. His paper is a medical landmark. It is apparently the earliest positive opinion in modern medicine of transcendental states of consciousness. Dr. Bucke defined three stages of consciousness: (1) simple consciousness (some animals); (2) Self consciousness (the British romantic poets on an ego trip); (3) Cosmic consciousness (Jesus, Buddha, Paul, Plotinus, Mohammed, Dante, Blake, and Walt Whitman).

Dr. Bucke's study was motivated also by his own experience with ultraconsciousness which is recounted in the preface to the 1974 edition of *Cosmic Consciousness*. Riding home in a cab while visiting England, he was

> in a state of quiet, almost passive enjoyment. All at once, without warning of any kind, he found himself wrapped around as it were by a flame-colored cloud. For an instant he thought of fire, some sudden conflagration in the great city; the next, he knew that the light was within himself. Directly afterwards came upon him a sense of exultation, of immense joyousness accompanied or immediately followed by an intellectual illumination quite impossible to describe .... He claims that he learned more within the few seconds during which the illumination lasted than in previous months or years of study, and that he learned much that no study could ever have taught.

Cosmic Consciousness itself is a series of case studies of historical figures and Bucke's contemporaries who had experienced the mystical state. Through omission this work tends to deny the extensive feminine experience in transcendence.

Dr. Bucke's contribution to the understanding of the mystical experience rather immediately inspired the pioneer American psychologist, William James, to give a famous lecture series, later published as *Varieties of Religious Experience* (1902). While this work contains many cases, it gives greater evidence of systematic analysis of ultraconsciousness. James repeatedly alludes to the medical materialists of his day who regarded the mystical experience as physiological in origin. This suggests that Dr. Bucke's positive attitude was somewhat unusual in the medical circles of that day. In fact, the next truly positive analysis in psychiatric circles would be an essay by the psychiatrist, Dr. Arthur J. Deikman, whose "De-automatization and the Mystic Experience" appeared in *Psychiatry* in 1966. Dr. Deikman began the task of salvaging the transcendent state from Freud's materialistic conception of it as "a memory of a relatively undifferentiated infantile ego state." At the 1972 meeting of the American Psychiatric

Association Dr. Stanley R. Dean also presented a very positive paper, "The Psychic Mystique—A Challenge to Science" which first introduced the term ultraconsciousness. Because of its neutrality (in terms of religious dogma) the term allows a more objective analysis of the topic.

All serious contemporary work on ultraconsciousness takes its departure from James' *Varieties of Religious Experience*. In this seminal work we see a scholar, a psychologist, and an historian of the psychology of the religious experience. The appearance of his book also represents the first counter-attack on Victorian materialism whose influence continued for decades in Freudian psychology. The practical consequence of these philosophic and scientific debates is that even to the present moment many psychiatrists tend to see mental illness in patients who have experienced ultraconsciousness. We regard this as a tragedy of both cultural and personal dimensions. In James' own day at Harvard he himself was of course surrounded by Victorian rationalism. For this reason, his investigation of mysticism invoked much hostility, as did his pioneering in the field later to be called parapsychology. Nonetheless, James openly attacks the medical materialism around him. He recognizes that the mystical experience might possibly be related to physical and mental disorders, yet nonetheless finds it a worthwhile subject of investigation.

The mystical experience has its origins in the "subliminal" (Freud's subconsious, Jung's Unconscious). Therefore its results must be authenticated through rational analysis. James further recognizes that such experiences carry a powerful authority of their own, thus testing and analysis of them is made difficult. James puts it:

> As a matter of psychological fact, mystical states of a well-pronounced and emphatic sort are usually authoritative over those who have had them. "Mystics" have been there and know it is vain for rationalism to grumble about this. If the mystical truth that comes to a man proves to be a force that he can live by, what mandate have we of the majority to order him to live in another way? . . . Our

own more rational beliefs are based on evidence exactly
similar in nature to that which mystics quote for theirs.

James' pragmatic acceptance of authentic inner experience
not demonstrably pathological is in marked contrast to the
majority of psychological and psychiatric opinion for half
a century afterwards.

Another point which James makes is that the mystical
experience transcends intellectual constructs such as religious
or philosophical systems. "The fact is that the mystical
feeling of enlargement, union, and emancipation has no
specific intellectual content, whatever of its own." James
works empirically toward such generalizations from many
causes. Bucke's work had prepared the way, but James
brought a more systematic mind to bear on this exotic
material. Fortunately *Varieties of Religious Experience* has
been kept in print by Modern Library; thus the reader who
can weather the Victorian prose will have his reward: an
enriched understanding of the varieties of ultraconsciousness.
Here, too, a more objective balance between the sexes is
represented in the choice of cases.

Those who may wish to update James' work may easily
do so with a contemporary title, *American Mysticism:
From William James to Zen* (1970) by Hal Bridges. If
pressed for time, sample the riches of present-day mysticism
in Bridge's chapter four. Here Bridges examines the inner
lives of three gifted men: Howard Thurman, a black theologian and religious leader; Abraham Heschel, a Jewish
mystic, and Thomas Merton, late Catholic monk and writer.
Aside from their distribution by faith, they also represent
the range and depth of contemporary mysticism.

The reader will recall that, according to James, ultraconsciousness renders the mystic invulnerable. The mystical experience has given Thurman invulnerability against
racial prejudice. As Bridges puts it, "Today Thurman is
an elder statesman of American religion, and on the surface
his record of achievement gives little indication of barriers
or cruel blows that racial discrimination deals against
human dignity." Bridges distinguishes between the surface

of Thurman's life (author of 15 books, guest lecturer at Harvard, Boston University Professor of Spiritual Discipline and Resources, and co-founder and pastor of The Church for the Fellowship of All People in San Francisco), and the attacks of discrimination. Thurman began his 1961 lecture at Baltimore Friends School with the statement that the inner light [through ultraconsciousness] was his fortress against racial discrimination.

Bridges quotes an experience of Thurman's from *Disciplines of the Spirit* (1963) which allows us to see one individual's preparation for ultraconsciousness:

> As a child I was accustomed to spend many hours in my rowboat, fishing along the river where there is no sound save the lapping of waves against the boat. There were times when it seemed as if the earth and the river and the sky and I were *one* beat of the same pulse. It was a time of watching and waiting for what I did not know—yet I always knew there would come a moment when beyond the single pulse beat there was a sense of Presence which always seemed to speak to me. My response to the sense of Presence always had the quality of personal communion. There was no voice. There was no image. There was no vision. There was God.

Then Bridges quotes a passage from Heschel's *God in Search of Man* (1955) which reminds us that it is the soul within us (Emerson's ''me''; Jung's ''Self''), that is the cosmic communications link: ''Man's walled mind has no access to a ladder upon which he can, on his own strength, rise to knowledge of God. Yet his soul is endowed with translucent windows that open to the beyond. And if he rises to reach out to Him, it is a reflection of the divine light in him that gives him the power for such yearning.'' When this mechanism is functioning, Heschel tells us in *Man Is Not Alone* (1951) the ultraconscious state flashes upon us:

> But then a moment comes like a thunderbolt in which a flash of the undisclosed rends our dark apathy asunder. It is full of overpowering brilliance, like a point in which all moments of life are focussed, or a thought which outweighs

all thoughts ever conceived of. There is so much light in our cage, in our world, it is as if it were suspended amidst the stars. Apathy turns to splendor unawares. The ineffable has shuddered itself into the soul . . . . We are penetrated by His insight. We cannot think anymore as if He were there and we here. He is both there and here. He is not a being but *being in any beyond all things* . . . a cry unrested from our very core, fills the world around us, as if a mountain were suddenly about to place itself in front of us. It is one word: God. Not an emotion, a stir within us, but a power, a marvel beyond us, tearing the world apart. The word that means more than universe, more than eternity, Holy, holy, holy; we cannot comprehend it. We only know it means infinitely more than we are able to echo.

Heschel's language evokes the original sense of the word "awe"; he makes obvious the limits of language when it attempts to recount ultraconsciousness.

To round out this impressionistic survey of American mysticism, we will conclude with the following passage from Merton's autobiography, *Seven Story Mountain* (1952):

But what a thing it was, this awareness: it was so intangible, and yet it struck me like a thunderclap. It was a light that was so bright that it had no relation to any visible light and so profound and so intimate that it seemed like a neutralization of every lesser experience. And yet the thing that struck me most of all was that this light was, in a certain sense "ordinary"—it was a light (and this most of all was what took my breath away) that was offered to all, to everybody and there was nothing fancy or strange about it. It was the light of faith deepened and reduced to a sudden and extreme obviousness. It was as if I had suddenly been illuminated by being blinded by the manifestation of God's Presence.

Obviously the power and the glory of each individual which Golding wrote of in his *Free Fall* is his universal and innate capacity for the illumination of ultraconsciousness.

In 1973 one of us gave a paper at the annual meeting of the American Psychiatric Association which was entitled, "The Ultraconscious State: A Natural Development of the

Psyche.'' It was intended as a contribution toward the re-discovery of the value of this ancient experience. The paper included two cases of ultraconsciousness taken from our own counselling.

We have already explained that we see this state of consciousness as a culmination of personal growth, a development which carries the individual beyond what he could hope to achieve on his own. Because of this the threat which this state poses to the ego (unless it is truly healthy) is enormous. It is well known that Western investigators from Freud to contemporary humanistic psychologists have given much attention to the ego. Perhaps as a consequence, to the present moment Western culture gives indications of being locked into those stages of consciousness dominated by the ego: the second (sex) and the third (power). Thus the full impact of Jung's discoveries has yet to reach the Western mind, still apparently fixated on Freud's undeniable contributions and other ego problems.

When the meaning of Jung's work is recognized, the importance of his having conceptualized the phase beyond ego development will be seen. This second stage, usually occurring in the second half of life, takes its departure from the achievement of a fully functional ego, itself a difficult project. The second stage involves the ego's awareness of something higher, the Self as Jung called it, or in *Memories, Dreams, Reflections* (1963), the soul. This term appears to be identical to the term used by the late Italian psychiatrist, Dr. Roberto Assagioli. Once the ego takes cognizance of the Self, the ultraconscious state becomes more probable. This second stage of individuation is thus a shift of focus from the transient personality to the more timeless Self. To find the Self, one goes within, typically because of the ego's pain in the outer world. In more general terms, this pain, associated with the major crisis of individuation contributes to a reorientation. The individual's goals shift from cultural and biological ends to spiritual concerns. Put another way, enough ego anguish will precipitate the night journey of the soul which, when successful, leads to the ego's conscious awareness of the Self.

While individuation is a perfectly normal and natural growth sequence, it does involve a threat to the ego—hence to personal stability. As Jung said in his "Commentary on 'The Secret of the Golden Flower' " (*Complete Works,* XIII). "The way is not without danger. Everything good is costly, and the development of personality is one of the most costly of all things." For this reason it is clear that the Western preoccupation with the ego is justified. Until the ego becomes truly healthy, the experience of ultra-consciousness can overwhelm it. The ego identifies with the Self (the Christ consciousness within) and says, "I am God." This is one psychological explanation of the psychotic state. It will be recalled that there is but a thin line between the genius and the madman. The slow process of authentic personal growth insures the ego stability needed for the state of ultraconsciousness.

We have already talked about the erratic personal behavior which ensues when the kundalini energy is aroused too suddenly instead of pursuing a slower and more controlled approach. In other words, for those who wish to grow, it is best to seek the middle ground. We will make practical suggestions in an appendix but the middle ground is somewhere between the promises of "weekend satori" made by some consciousness-raising workshops and Jung's view of the Unconscious as an almost totally autonomous mechanism regulating growth outside of the individual's conscious control. For now, let us say that one begins with this recognition: however pleasant and fulfilling it may be to the ego, existence at the sex and power levels is an incomplete expression of our potential. To put it another way, continued major expenditure of psychic energy in these activities of consciousness deprive one of realizing the full potential of the psyche.

Unfortunately, many will stop their growth once they achieve a healthy ego. Since it is only through the Self that transpersonal awareness becomes possible—i.e., an exit from the mirror walls of the ego's solitary cell into a truly creative relation with the cosmos—failure to achieve such wholeness not only limits the individual but mankind as well. In other words, the stakes for which we play justify the ego risk. To avoid risk is to become static. When growth ceases, death begins. Many personalities die long before the physical organism ceases to function.

Earlier in this chapter we suggested a change of society's attitudes toward ultraconsciousness. The consequence is that we are privileged to share an ever increasing variety of the inner experiences of others. As a result, those who now have such experiences can find them fulfilling instead of frightening. One of the subjects whose case we will share below spent years doubting her own sanity after her initial breakthrough into transcendent realms. Yet today leaders of public opinion are beginning to admit such experiences publicly.

In 1967, David Snell, a senior editor of *Life* magazine recounted his near-fatal reaction to penicillin and the ensuing transcendent encounter in an article "How It Feels To Die" (May 26). As he passed over the threshold from life to death, Mr. Snell sensed a love so exhalting in its effect upon him that at the time he was disappointed to be pulled away from it by the medical treatment that saved his life. The blind singer-composer Stevie Wonder, injured in an automobile accident in 1973, told the press of an out-of-body experience of ultraconsciousness: "The only thing I do know is that I was unconscious and that I was definitely, for a few days, in a much better spiritual place that made me aware of a lot of things that concern my life and my future and what I have to do to reach another higher ground." Sharing such experiences with a mass audience surely has helped the average person to react with more understanding.

The first case is that of June who is fully functional by all standards of which we are aware. She is married, has five children and has successfully coped with mental illness in a member of the family. She has held the number two post in a large electronic firm and has completed a master's degree. She is now a candidate for the Ph.D. in her chosen field. In other words, by most standards she is a fully functional person. In her own words she tells of her own experiences in the ultraconscious state. She also seeks to explain differing levels of this state:

There are different levels of this ultraconscious experience, all of which fit the description, yet are quite different in themselves. I have experienced two, one a true summit, or at least *a* summit, one time sixteen years ago, plus a similar experience during the past four years. I shall try to differentiate between the levels.

Sixteen years ago [at the age of thirty], completely spontaneously, I was transported to a summit. I suppose the experience might sound "suspicious" to some, for it did happen in a church; however, the setting had nothing to do with the incident. The choir was progressing and I was singing the old standard "Holy, Holy, Holy," that had become meaningless through repetition. In tact, I was looking over the congregation and trying to get ideas for some sort of spring outfit (I had four babies under the age of five, and a fifth one was born either a few weeks before or after this event, I have never been able to remember the exact day it occurred). At any rate I needed a new dress rather badly. In one step, I did not falter in the processional, yet I experienced an endless transformation. Time and space ceased to be; I was in a limitless pale blue void, bathed in the most inexpressible light. There was joy, but so far beyond joy that it was not joy; it was not ecstasy, there was *no* emotion, for it was too far beyond emotion of any sort . . . primarily, it was a "knowing"; I knew that all the Universe was there and so far beyond man's comprehension that he could not even comprehend that he could not comprehend, yet all knowledge was there. I realized that were I even to try to grasp any of this immersion I would be totally destroyed, but this was not at all in fear, there was no fear, nothing but knowledge, and understanding of the whole that has left me saying these years past, "It simply doesn't matter" which requires much explanation for which there is no room here. This was an endless period. In a sense it is still with me, yet in our time sense it must have been less than a tenth of a second. The light was within me, yet I was "looking" at it. It was a union so complete there was

no sense of union as we use the word, and I was more completely my individual self than ever in this world. All words
are meaningless . . . they simply do not express in any way
what happened. I repeat, there was no ecstasy, no emotion;
the sense of triumph, joy, grandeur, awe, wonder were all
carried to an extreme that nullified them; there was no
room for anything but "knowing" . . . pure intellect, pure
light was all.

A year or so ago June had another experience of ultraconsciousness of a "lesser nature." The incident has the
additional interest of being directly related to the out-of-
body experience. June's first out-of-body experience had
occurred in surgery. Afterwards the surgeon was surprised
to hear her description of the operation from high in the
operating room. Here is the second event:

> I was deliberately trying to travel out of the body one night,
> about 2:00 a.m. I did, apparently dissociate and there was
> the sense of another entity present; This second "person"
> extended a "hand" toward me as in fellowship, and suddenly
> there was the dazzling light that filled *our* being for we were
> one; yet, as before I was more my own individual, more
> completely me, than before. This time there was ecstasy, I
> did feel emotions, joy, awe, the understanding of the meaning
> of the universe especially was clearer, that is, more within
> my grasp than in the first instance. . . there was emotion
> beyond any real description as well as intellect in this ex-
> perience. Again, however, though ineffable, by comparison
> this was farther *below* the first than it was above normal
> daily life. Love, compassion and understanding of all were
> present.

June describes the second experience as "analogous, although very remotely, to erotic love and expressed as a
highly evolved transmutation of sex vitality." The first
experience, in contrast, was too far beyond human experience to be compared with it. A third event, similar to
the second may also be of interest to the reader:

[This one] occurred in full daylight one afternoon . . . . A person who was talking to me cried out, with real anxiety, "Oh, if you could only *know*, if you could only know!" and suddenly there was a sensation of inner light and I did know; I was, literally "looking" at myself through the other's eyes, feeling the other's body around me, and knowing the thoughts that were spinning in the other mind. This was all an overlay to my own consciousness. It was as though I was one with the other person. This last was a much lesser experience, related to the others only in the difficulty of expression, the sensation of light, (not so great as in the others) in the understanding of wider concepts, in the suspension of time and space, and in the "unity," this time with just one other being. This I would not call a summit, however.

The difference in level, then, I would say is in the presence of ecstasy, and the human time element. I did not mention it, but the second experience, while without time or space, lasted approximately twenty minutes our time. The true summit completely obliterated time in our sense.

Although, for all accounts, such experiences may highlight an ongoing inner development pattern, they may also be the break in a psychic drought which may also have included the night journey of the soul. Such experiences then appear to function as the pivotal point for a turnaround, or a psychic life buoy for the individual until he is able to restore the harmony of his outer life.

Many of us are like pilots of small aircraft, hurtling through zero visibility weather without a radio, bumping around in the soup, anxiously looking through a rain-smeared windshield, and all the while trusting to an old compass. After the experience of ultraconsciousness, we may fly through the same weather but we are following more sophisticated instruments. We depart under instrument flight rules but our destination is under visual flight rules with ceiling unlimited.

All this is true *if* the person who has the experience possesses a framework or a tradition in which to place it. If not, he may suffer as did Jane whose case we discussed in chapter two. At this point it may be helpful to recount

one of Jane's experiences with ultraconsciousness, the out-
of-body event which occurred at the age of twenty-nine. At
a crisis in her marriage, she was sitting in a parked automobile talking with another man. They were returning from
night teaching assignments:

> [Suddenly she found herself] outside the car, standing in
> mid-air, about even with the hinges on the door. I was
> standing just above the level of the hood. There was a man
> on my left. He had on a white robe-type thing—I never did
> turn and look at him. I was aware that he was standing
> beside me. I could see him out of the corner of my eye.
> There wasn't anything unusual about it. I wasn't afraid
> when it happened. [Jane, during the previous two months,
> realizing the need for outside help, had spent much time in
> prayer and reading about Christ's life.] I wasn't afraid
> because—he didn't have to tell me who he was but I knew
> that the man standing next to me was Christ, and what he
> said to me will bear that out. I was watching myself sit-
> ting in the car behind the wheel . . . the sensation was like
> being in a room conversing with someone with
> the television on. I was aware of what I was doing
> but it was unimportant, just like the television would be
> unimportant if there were one on here right now. And I
> didn't hear anything with my physical ears. It was a sort
> of telepathic communication. And he said, "You are going
> to have this one day, anyway, don't ruin it now." [Ap-
> parently the love of the man with her.] And I saw a
> scene from what I would take to be the future. [In the
> scene, she feels intense joy and is in a prayer of thanksgiv-
> ing; the scene was apparently precognitive as it is descriptive
> of her inner life at the present writing, some ten years later.
> In a second scene she was in her forties and sitting on the
> edge of a bed with someone else. As she viewed these scenes,
> she heard] "All I'm asking is that you keep my command-
> ments and trust me, that's all I'm asking, that you trust
> me" . . . and—bam—I was back inside my body. There was
> no sensation of either leaving or coming back . . . .

This experience and the two that followed for Jane ultimately, as we earlier noted, both enriched and guided her life—

some years after, when she came to understand their meaning. In the interval between, she agonized over her own sanity; after all, the society she lived in would consider her inner life indicative of mental illness. It took a university lecture which placed ultraconsciousness in the tradition to fit her experiences into a meaningful pattern.

We have tried to hint at the limitless variety of inner riches which have come to mankind in those moments at which the temple within has been flooded with cosmic light. Despite the infinite spectrum, four key characteristics are manifested. These were most notably stated by William James in his *Variety of Religious Experience*. First of all, the event has "ineffability"; "it defies expression" and relates more to the emotions than the intellect. "Lacking the heart or ear, we cannot interpret the musician or the lover justly, and are even likely to consider him weak-minded or absurd. The mystic finds that most of us accord to his experiences an equally incompetent treatment." Second, such incidents have a "noetic quality"; that is, despite their close relation to emotional experience, they also contain knowledge beyond the limitations of rational thought, knowledge which carries its own authority. Third, the state exhibits "transiency." Despite its evanescence, however, the mystical state when repeated builds a powerful inner life. Fourth, the state is characterized by "passivity." However active the preparation might have been, the will is set aside for the duration of the experience: "the mystic feels as if his own will were in abeyance, and indeed sometimes as if he were grasped and held by a superior power."

Also, despite the infinite permutations of the ultraconscious state, two overall patterns are evident: (1) Deliberate willed efforts to grow in preparation for ultraconsciousness often precede the event, and (2) a spontaneous "conversion" experience falls upon the person who is totally unprepared for it. This latter is far less common, and from its described impact in the more dramatic cases, something of threat to the ego's stability. Of course, sometimes as we have suggested earlier the ego requires a shake-up.

We have given the reader cases of the spontaneous route.

They should be helpful to those readers who may themselves
know it first hand. As for active preparation, it might be
well to summarize the various suggestions which have been
accumulating in our description of the temple within. He
who actively seeks the temple is using the will in a way
which leads to harmony. By contrast, the use of the will at
the level of sex or power makes for disharmony, even if a
necessary part of growth. Here, the ego is looking out for
itself. Below are, as we see it, the positive tasks of will:

(1) Physical discipline of the body to prepare a fully functional vehicle which will not of itself retard the experience. This includes diet, exercise, and, ultimately,
purification—within some body of knowledge about fasting. Experimenting with fasting without specific advice
is not recommended.

(2) The on-going task of individuation. While much tran-
spires in the Unconscious, practical conscious efforts
toward growth contribute to individuation. Increasing
self-awareness, if relatively objective in its nature, contribute. The goal is the achievement of sufficient ego
strength to weather the major crisis of individuation.
This includes learning to be fully functional at the lower
levels of consciousness. The study of one's dreams is
an important part of this approach. (See the appendices
for additional suggestions.)

(3) Mental discipline. This aspect may perhaps be the one
which is most clearly understood in the West. Yet some
important considerations have been out of fashion for a
time. This area of preparation ranges from knowledge
of the wonders of the physical universe as it is now beginning to be understood by science to recognition of
man's spiritual nature and the essential mystery of the
cosmos. Apprehension of these latter will be but an in-
intellectual and vicarious process until ultraconsciousness
itself.

The will may also be employed to another end: the will
may will to abdicate. This at least temporarily is the result
of conscientiously followed meditation practices. In tradition-

al language it is this deliberate choice: "Not my will, but Thine. . . ." Looked at another way, the active steps suggested above are the most valid preparation for meditation.

Once ultraconsciousness is known, how does one validate or test it? James recognized the great difficulty in so doing. Brad Steiger, in his *Revelation: The Divine Fire* (1973), has an excellent chapter, "Testing the Validity of the Divine Fire." Here he quotes a fine comment by Diane Kennedy Pike:

> My personal feeling is that the test Jesus gave is really the safest one, and that is that you really can know the difference by the person's life. I think that a person who has received a revelation from the Higher Realm will manifest high characteristics or qualities in his life and understanding. There will emerge in him a deeper sense of peace as a result of his communication and a deeper sense of wholeness. Physical health will begin to manifest. He will show great patience, speak of universal laws, and give evidence of the things that Paul calls the fruits of the spirit.
>
> I think a person who is on his own mental trip will manifest what we call ego qualities, which is a kind of deceptiveness, self-assertiveness, pride, and so forth, which are not really characteristics of higher developed spiritual people.

Steiger also reminds us of the succinct tests posed by Dr. Raynor C. Johnson (*Watcher on the Hills*, 1959):

(1) The pragmatic test. Has it led to well-balanced, happy, serene living of an enhanced quality?

(2) Is it *consistent* with the well-established findings of reason? (This need not imply that it is *supported* by reason.)

(3) Is it unifying and integrative, or isolating and destructive so far as the individual's relationship to an all-embracing whole is concerned?

In short, authentic ultraconsciousness produces changes in the individual which make him more joyous, more loving and hence more harmonious. Also, the individual then seeks to share the illumination he has found within the temple. If the revelation as been authentic, he will be especially moved to share this essential truth: The mystery is within; each must go into the temple himself. This is the essence of the unfolding Aquarian Age.

Appendix One

"A Case of Personality Reversal"

At a recent workshop in which we participated, the following case was shared which, in the spirit of William James, shows an instantaneous "conversion" with positive an demonstrable benefits to personality. In this case, the Self was receiving tutoring which was unknown to the conscious mind until its contents became strong enough to break through, thus transforming behavior and orientation. Here we see more of the phenomenal power of the Unconscious, influenced by the energy of others, to be sure, yet serving as a link to that which Cayce called the Supraconscious. We refer back to Carl Jung's work "The Transcendent Function" (1916) to show that while consciousness inhibits material which is incompatible with its desires, the purpose of the Unconscious is to compensate. This is another case which demonstrates help for an individual beyond his conscious will.

Mr. S. describes his problem as follows:

I had been drinking and smoking since I was about fifteen. At first, I guess I started because I wanted to be "an adult." I continued it for kicks and because of a certain amount of peer-group pressure. By the time I was 21 or 22 I really wanted to quit both habits—but I just could not. I really felt inferior because I just didn't have the Will to stop. So I said, "The hell with it—" and went at drinking like it was the only way of life. Over the next 18 or 19 years, I drank more

143

and more and liked it less and less but still could not stop.
It was when I was about 39 that my wife started going to
Alanon—the group that helps the familes of Alcoholics. I
guess I vaguely remember her going but didn't think I was
an alcoholic.

Mr. S. relates that about this time his wife left books about
the house about Edgar Cayce and some by Emmet Fox.
He had not attended church since he was around twelve,
but felt attracted to these books and read them. Still he
could not stop drinking. Change was coming, however.

> All I can now surmise is that—my wife, and my mother, must
> have been praying correctly and seeing the presence of God
> where my trouble seemed to be—because one afternoon when
> I was in "my" tavern starting to get "half a load on"(I was
> suddenly struck with a marvelous feeling that drinking was
> stupid and that I was to stop. Now, I had known intellec-
> tually for a long time that drinking was stupid but at this
> moment I knew it with power—and I knew I had absolutely
> *no desire* to drink—then or ever again. It was really a
> fantastic feeling to be sitting in a bar already half-loaded
> and know that you were in reality no longer in the grips of
> alcohol. I remember saying good-bye to the bartender and
> telling him I wouldn't be in again. I guess he must have
> laughed at that one. I'm sure he's heard it before and
> since. But for me, it was the truth.

Later that night he told his wife that he was through with
drinking and thanked her for her prayers. They had the
first really free and open talk together which they had had
in years. The next day Mr. S. realized that he no longer
wanted or needed cigarettes. As he started to light one first
thing in the day, something in him said, "That's another
stupid thing. You don't need it. That's out of your life for-
ever." He remembers saying "Thank God," the first real
prayer he had said in years. He was afraid of telling his
wife of this and then slipping back but after three weeks
she noticed that his carton of cigarettes did not need re-
plenishing. He told her, "I don't smoke anymore—haven't
for three weeks"; and he "knew again in that moment

the same power I had felt when I was in that bar—a feeling of control and confidence that was not of myself, and I knew that God had helped me.''

Mr. S. realizes that it was not his personal will but a power outside of him which saved him from these disintegrating habits. He advises others to switch their desires to the will of the Divine each time a habit tries to impose itself. Shifting from the personal will into the viewpoint of the higher Self, the divine in you, is necessary. Learn to do it, have a desire to succeed, and it will steer you from all the dangerous by-ways and emotional, mental and physical detours.

Appendix Two

"Psychointegration: Suggestions for
Personal Development"

What can you do for yourself in this system of personality? Keeping in mind that the major events of individuation are sometimes beyond the conscious control of the will, you can begin by attending to the development of a healthy ego in preparation for the inner growth of the second half of life. Such preparation will be vital if the transition is marked by a major crisis.

1. Become aware of your own ego defense mechanisms. (When you are strongly judgmental about another person, is it because of something within yourself that you don't like, yet haven't looked at very candidly?)

2. Gradually circumventing these mechanisms as much as possible, begin to accept more responsibility for your own actions.

3. Recognize the extent to which you are *presently* programmed by outer events, circumstances and so on, *rather* than by your own developmental needs. (Granted, earlier circumstances, such as one's childhood, are difficult to reconstruct on your own.)

4. Identify the major thrust of your personality: i.e., the levels of consciousness at which your energies seem to be focussed. Probably it is more or less appropriate to your age, but, should you wish to try to accelerate your growth, remember that the unfolding of personality is a slow, subtle

process requiring much patience. One particularly demanding part of the process results from what may be manifested as erratic behavioral patterns when the psyche's energies begin to refocus as a new level. The ego is, of course, (sometimes painfully) learning a new role. Thus each level calls for a rebalancing of body, mind and spirit. Progress may not even be sequential; often it is not. Nor are the levels to be thought of as watertight compartments. As in biological evolution, you carry with you the vestiges of the earlier levels. What is significant is your *own* recognition of the focus of your consciousness *and* your own evaluation of your development in relation to your life goals. The extent to which you may wish to develop is entirely your own affair. Many will be fully effective, even fulfilled personalities at the fourth level (heart and compassion). From the viewpoint of society, the appearance of greater numbers of people functioning at the fourth level would have great positive impact, particularly in interpersonal relations. In regard to the upper levels, while all have the potential for such growth, not all will consider it desirable. On the other hand, in our opinion this is no reason to avoid a full description of mankind's potential. In every age there are those who choose to discipline themselves for inner growth; consequently while all have the same potential, only a few illustrate that potential in their lives. It is fashionable in some circles today to call this "elitist" thinking; such a label belongs in politics and sociology. In consciousness its only possible application is to one guilty of spiritual pride. If the charge of elitism is used to deny the existence of levels of inner growth, it represents ignorance of the facts and is a disservice to the race.

5. Be *patient* with all these insights; recognize them *not* as faults but as *unfinished psychological business*. Do not spin in with morbid introspection. Instead, let intellectual awareness and insights work into the Unconsciousness naturally. Remember that the Unconscious has its own self-correcting mechanisms.

6. Recognize the utility of Dr. Viktor E. Frankl's existential freedom—the freedom to find valid meanings within

existing circumstances, if these circumstances are, for the time being, unalterable.

7. Make a serious study of your dreams in order to gain more insight into what your ego must call the Unconscious.

8. Work toward the balancing of the modes of cognition: i.e., if a feeling mode type, seek the discipline of the mind with the facts of outer reality; if a thinking type, add experiences which will call forth a richer emotional existence. (Note: We do not mean greater subjectivity or intensification of the cruder emotional responses.) Charles Darwin, lamenting the rational set of his scientific life, said that, if he had it to do over again, he would listen to music and read poetry each week. Identification with the cruder emotions is counterproductive. Ouspensky spoke of the need to separate oneself from such emotions. Say not "I am angry" but "I am being overtaken by anger."

9. In the inevitable suffering from the rejection of the ego in the many inflation-rejection cycles, make an effort each time for a glimpse of objectivity. Was the ego inflated in relation to your real capacity? Thus the rejection can be taken as an occasion for growth.

10. With increasing awareness, begin to distinguish between that suffering which is both inevitable and productive of growth and that suffering which is self-inflicted (i.e., neurotic).

11. Failure or paralysis of will may accompany a neurosis. While various therapeutic techniques may blast one off of dead center, it is in the small day-to-day triumphs over our imperfections, the gradual alteration of a destructive outlook, and the slow training of the indolent animal we inhabit that our evolution towards wholeness is affected. In this respect evolution includes the development toward autonomy and away from a paralysis of will: one is less and less a slave of the emotions (including ego-related emotions) and less and less a slave of circumstances.

12. Keep a journal as a means to growth for the following reasons:

    1. It develops objectivity toward momentary enthusiasms.

2. It develops an awareness of the evolutionary pattern of one's life.

3. If dreams are recorded and analyzed, one has access to the vital territory of the Unconscious—and its development.

4. In retrospect the journal may help one to recognize newly emerging stages of growth. Long entries may give a clue. Significant dreams may also serve to alert to change. Too, events may cluster in significant ways. It is important to recognize the difference between the rationalization of the ego (an ego defense mechanism) and rational thought (particularly the higher rationality of psychointegration).

13. Work toward reasonable physical discipline and fitness, including a proper diet for your particular needs. This need not be an athletic endeavor. Hatha yoga accomplishes much for the body with relatively light energy consumption.

14. Practice some system of regular meditation daily, if only for 15-30 minutes. The major benefit at first will be a balancing out of the effects of external programming of the personality. Ultimately the cosmic awareness which will provide an authentic basis for brotherly love will come. The philosophic materialist tends toward I-it relations.

15. If available, seek the guidance of someone who has preceded you on this path but remember that success or failure is your own doing.

16. The more whole we become, the more we can help others. The fourth level, heart and compassion, suggests both a developing sensitivity to others' needs *and* an evolving capacity to meet those needs. One is no longer merely coping with his or her own personal needs.

Caution Notice:

While the psyche usually protects one from pursuits which will overwhelm it, it should be stated plainly that the active path of growth herein outlined may be too demanding for some. For them it would be wise to let nature take her course.

Appendix Three

"A Personal and Historical Note on Psychointegration"

Nineteen years ago I was struck by the narrow view of man in the psychological literary criticisms I encountered in my graduate studies. Freud's sexual determinism seemed to reduce man's infinite range of possibilities to but varieties of sexual behavior. This initiated a search for a more comprehensive psychology. As a student of the Victorian period, I came to see the ultimate sterility to which the rationalism of the day led. This, of course, was the intellectual climate from which Freud's sexual determinism emerged. I dealt at length with this topic in a book, *Leslie Stephen* (1972). The options which began to emerge even in graduate school were Carl Jung, Ralph Waldo Emerson, and the influences upon Emerson—Plotinus, the *Bhagavad Gita* and others. Jung's understanding of the Unconscious seemed preferable to Freud's reduction of it to a sort of psychic garbage can.

Through the years I found other important insights in the work of Dr. Victor E. Frankl, Abraham Maslow, and Dr. Roberto Assagioli. Their work reinforced the instinct towards a more sophisticated model of the psyche and its growth patterns. David C. McClelland's work on a value psychology confirmed a feeling that value-free psychologies have no utility as growth models.

All of these tendencies were reinforced in years of

counselling students in crucial growth situations. Some-
time before 1973 I read Dick Alpert's (now Baba Ram
Dass) *Be Here Now* which explicity related the work of
Freud and Adler to the second and third chakras, which is
to say, the lower levels of consciousness. This confirmed
another instinct: that because of its youth, the West so far
has developed psychologies which are primarily relevant to
lower levels of consciousness—primarily those dominated by
the ego. In 1973 the connections I had added to Alpert's
were included in a paper presented as a discussant at a
panel given by the American Psychiatric Association in
Honolulu. This was the paper on Ultraconsciousness.

The product of this search is psychointegration, an ex-
tension of Jung's central concept—individuation—as elabor-
ated by Drs. Jolande Jacobi and Edward F. Edinger.
Psychointegration extends individuation by the additional
concept of growth related to levels of consciousness. These
levels, derived from Hindu physiology (the chakras, which,
despite Lawrence LeShan's statements, are not metaphors)
bring the Eastern influence into the system. This addition
to individuation makes it more useful for those in the
first half of the individuation process. It also allows us
to see the functional relationships of the various historical
schools of psychology in the West. Specific schools are
therefore related to the different growth stages of the psyche.
Thus, for example, the humanistic psychologies which have
evolved since 1945 would appear to represent a coming
transition of the Western ego to the heart and compassion
(or fourth chakra) level of consciousness. Current multi-
modal therapies represent a practical response to the phe-
nomenological evidence of the various growth stages.

Psychointegration is oriented towards growth and away
from pathology. Psychological disharmony is identified as
"unfinished business of the psyche." The system is quite
obviously a value psychology with a normative structure
comprehensive enough to include the peak experience of
ultraconsciousness within the normal human potential.

In recent years through various elaborations of psychointegration, it has assumed the character of a phi-

losophy of personality, judged by the usual criteria of philosophic thought. This is to say that the full development will probably occupy the rest of my life.

Jung said, "The reality of life, with all its abysses and terrors, its unpredictable qualities, cannot be covered by so-called 'clear concepts.' " He therefore deliberately sought ambiguity, despite his own temperamental inclination to unequivocal statement. In the psychological world, this still tends to make Jung caviar to the general. Freud, on the other hand, opted for a governing idea, sexuality. Consequently his view has dominated Western psychology for many years. However there are now signs of a desire for a middle ground. Perhaps psychointegration will contribute to that need.

D.D.Z.

Appendix Four

"Technical Notes on Kirlian Photography"

Our interest in Kirlian photography goes back to 1970 when Sheila Ostrander and Lynn Schroeder reported on their trip to various Soviet-bloc countries in *Psychic Discoveries Behind the Iron Curtain* (1970). Since that time they have also published their *Handbook of Psi Discoveries* (1974) which has several helpful chapters on Kirlian photography for those who may wish to begin their own experiment.

Our own research at Lamar University with our co-researcher Dr. Joseph Pizzo, Lamar physics professor, began in 1972 under the helpful guidance of the U.S. pioneer in Kirlian photography, U.C.L.A. physiologist, Dr. Thelma Moss. Professor Douglas Dean of the Newark College of Engineering and Dr. William Tiller, Stanford University physicist are also key figures in the early U.S. development of this Russian invention actually anticipated in 1885 in Philadelphia by Nikola Tesla. Dr. Moss' equipment was built by Kendall Johnson, Professor Dean's was brought from an Iron Curtain country, and Dr. Tiller has designed his own. Despite the extreme sophistication of Dr. Tiller's gear (actually because of it) he has failed to observe certain effects noted by Dr. Moss: changes of state in Kirlian photography from various psychic and physiological states. Dr. Tiller (until the middle of 1975) had been saying that corona discharge would account for the effects he had ob-

153

served. In a letter to *Psychic Magazine* (August 1975), Dr.
Tiller announced that Kirlian equipment operating in the
frequency range of 1-10 kilohertz would theoretically produce
the effects claimed by the others. He himself had been
working in the higher range of 100 kilohertz to 1 mega-
hertz and had yet to experiment at the lower frequencies.
Due to the availability of certain equipment, the Lamar
experiment began operating at 7.7 kilohertz. As a consequence, by 1974 we had replicated a number of Dr. Moss'
effects and added two of our own: an 8'' x 10'' Ektachrome profile of Dr. Pizzo's face which Dr. Moss has
verified as revealing acupuncture points and fingertip photographs of meditators as they concentrated in the different
chakras. The profile was included in Dr. Moss' film,
"Explorations in Kirlian Photography," which was shown at
The Second International Psychotronics Conference in
Monaco (1975).

The Lamar Kirlian project, now in its fourth year, has
been funded for two years by the Lamar Research Council.
The basic experiment designed by David Cammack has
four data points: the Kirlian photograph, the subject's
written description of his internal state (mental or physiological), and written accounts of two clairvoyants observing the subject's head and shoulder aura. The colors (clair-
voyantly observed versus Kirlian photographed) show little
correlation—this is probably due to the fact that we are
photographing fingertips and the clairvoyants are observing head and shoulders. On the other hand, changes
of state (diameter, structure, etc.) do seem to correlate
among the four data points. Furthermore, controlled
changes of state such as going in and out of hypnosis,
physiological alteration from radiation therapy do seem to
affect the Kirlian photo. These observations have satisfied
us that the Kirlian process is not just corona discharge but
corona discharge modulated by the energy field of the
subject. The technical characteristics which seem most productive (in addition to the 7.7 kilohertz operating frequency)
include a voltage of about 25 kilovolts, a one second exposure, and Ektacolor film. All normal high voltage pre-

cautions must be taken when working with such voltages. Above all, the set-up must make it impossible for the subject to be grounded or radio frequency burns may occur. Finally, we do not recommend replication of the profile experiment.

Recommended Reading

1. Assagioli, Roberto, M.D. *The Act of Will.* N.Y. Viking Press, 1973.
   A very practical approach to strengthening your will and making it "skillful" and constructive. Also a clear account of the principles of meditation.

2. Bridges, Hal. *American Mysticism; From William James to Zen*, N.Y. Harper & Row, 1970; CSA Press, 1977

3. Bro, Harmon, Ph.D. *Edgar Cayce on Dreams.* N.Y. Warner Communication, 1974.
   A psychologically sound account of the Cayce material on the value and meanings of dreams.

4. Brown Barbara, Ph.D. *New Mind, New Body; Bio-Feedback: New Directions for the Mind.* N.Y. Harper and Row, 1974.
   Excellent survey of contemporary works in bio-feedback and a clear statement of the meaning of this research for mankind.

5. Faraday, Ann, Ph.D. *Dream Power.* N.Y. Berkley Madallion Publishing Co. 1097.
   Another excellent guide to your dream life.

6. Progoff, Ira, Ph.D. *At A Journal Workshop.* N.Y. Dialogue House Library, 1975.
   As much as most will want to know about the mechanics and the benefits of journal keeping.

7. Roberts, Jane. *Seth Speaks.* Englewood Cliffs, N.J. Prentice-Hall, 1972.
   An extraordinarily broad teaching of a high spiritual order.

8. Schmidt, K.O. *Lao-Tse's Book of Life*, CSA Press, Lakemont, Ga. 1975.
   Beautiful introduction of ancient Chinese philosophy.

About the Author

David Zink was born in Kansas City, Missouri. He received a Bachelor of Journalism from the University of Colorado. Among other teaching experiences, he established a course at Lamar University in Beaumont, Texas called "Cosmologies: Ancient and Modern" which examined schools of Western psychology, Eastern philosophy, parapsychology and the world wide development of higher consciousness.

Joan Zink is an author, poet and composer whose work has appeared in many countries. Through years of meditation she has reached levels of consciousness, which facilitated her innate mysticism, healing abilities, and helped develop her powerful creative mind.